Mollie
Costarella

THE ALL COLOR BOOK OF
THE BODY

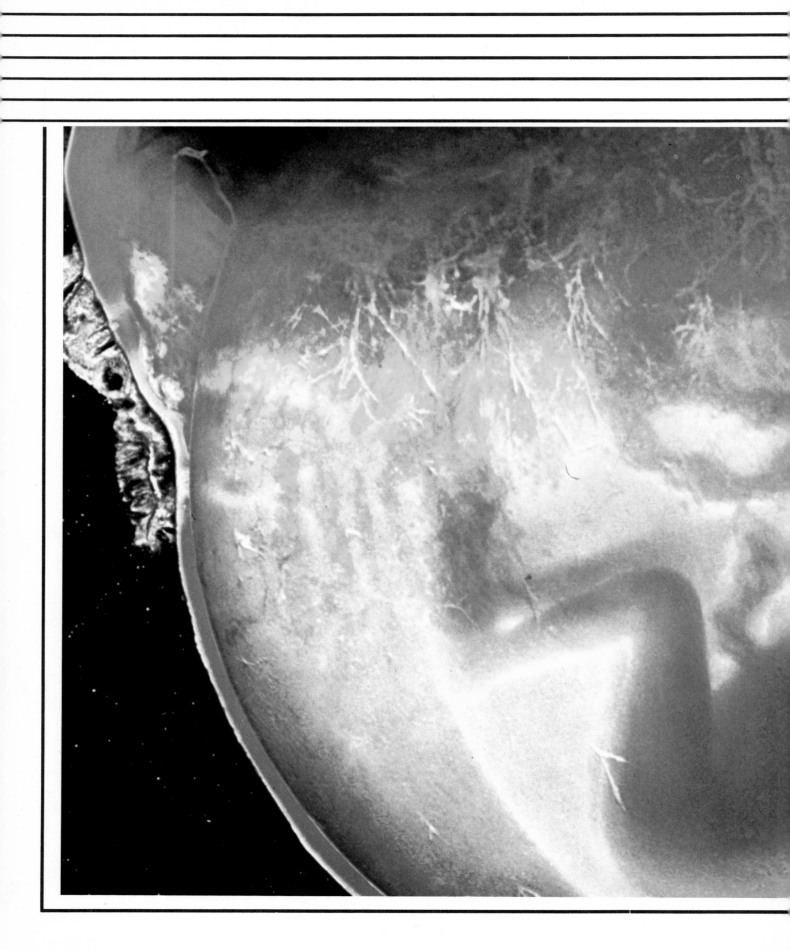

THE ALL COLOR BOOK OF
THE BODY

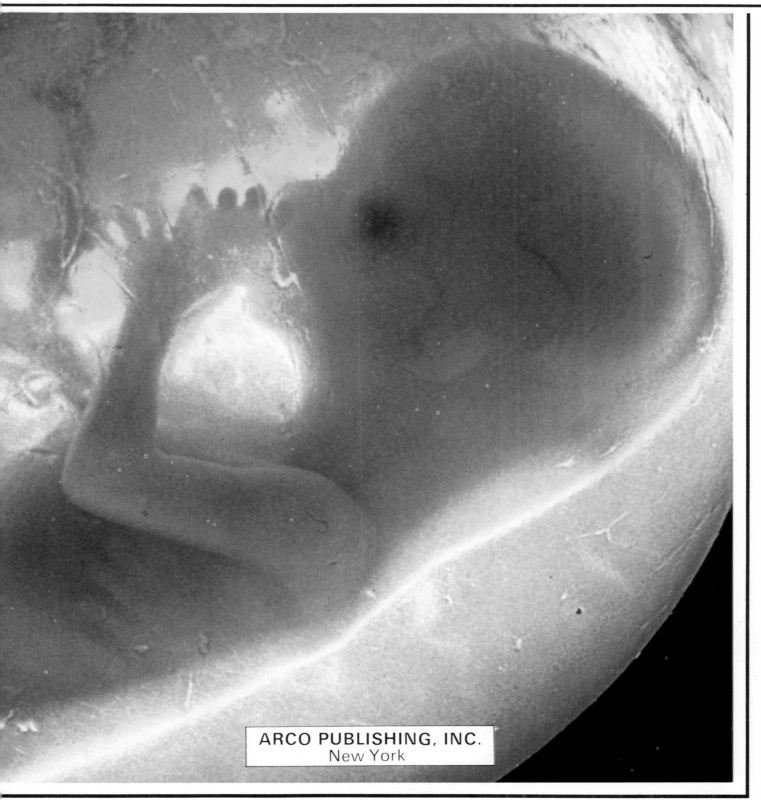

ARCO PUBLISHING, INC.
New York

Published by Arco Publishing, Inc.
215 Park Avenue South, New York, NY 10003

Library of Congress Cataloging in Publication Data
Main entry under title:

The All color book of the body.

   Includes index.
   Summary: Presents the parts of the human body,
including simple cells, tissues, organs, and systems
such as the nervous system.
   1. Anatomy, Human—Juvenile literature. 2. Body,
Human—Juvenile literature. (1. Anatomy, Human.
2. Body, Human)
QM27.A43   1985   611   84-29011
ISBN 0-668-06510-9

© Marshall Cavendish Limited 1985

Printed and bound in Hong Kong by
Dai Nippon Printing Company

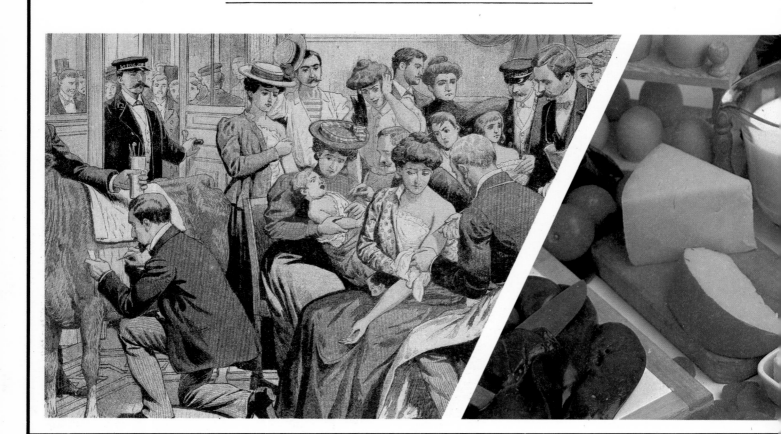

CONTENTS

INTRODUCTION

Below: A constant supply of oxygen and other materials is vital for the survival of the brain, the body's control centre. So, entangled with the dense network of nerve connections is the almost equally dense network of blood vessels shown by the resin cast.

Below centre: Runners setting off to run the 26-mile course of the New York marathon will soon stretch many of their body systems to the limit as heart and lungs work furiously to supply the hungry muscles with energy.

Every moment of the day, even while you sleep, your body is busy at work. Your chest is steadily pumping air in and out of your lungs. Your heart is squeezing powerfully away, sending blood shooting through the blood vessels. Chemical agents are at work in the intestine. Nerve signals are buzzing to and fro, speeding information from the senses to the brain and carrying instructions to all parts of the body. Chemical messengers are co-ordinating all kinds of activities.

All of these activities, however different they may seem, have the same purpose—to maintain your body. The simplest forms of life have just one cell and simply absorb food through the cell walls to preserve life. Human beings are infinitely more

complex, put together from billions of different cells. But as the single-cell organism works independently to preserve its life, so all the cells of the body work together to maintain the body. The body's cells can look very different, but each forms part of a special body system, and each of these systems works together. Some cells make up the body's fuelling system; others contribute to the monitoring system— the senses; others help in the task of co-ordination and control, and so on. But all these complex systems have the same purpose. So, although in this book the body is divided into various systems, it is worth remembering that they are really inseparably linked, working together to maintain the fragile balance of life.

Below: Some of the largest cells in the body are the nerve cells that control and monitor the body's activities. But even these cells are generally minute, visible only with the aid of a powerful electron microscope.

CHAPTER 1

FUELLING THE BODY

Like a machine, the body needs energy for all its actions. It also needs a constant supply of materials for growth and for replacing its own worn-out parts. Both these needs are met by food and drink—the fuels of the body— and oxygen. The blood acts as a transport system to carry the food and oxygen to the cells, where the food is burned to produce energy. Any waste products are then removed by the blood for disposal.

A cast made by injecting resin shows the millions of tiny, branching airways inside each of our two lungs. All these airways are needed to allow fresh oxygen from the air we breathe into the lungs to filter through into the blood; and to allow stale carbon dioxide to filter back.

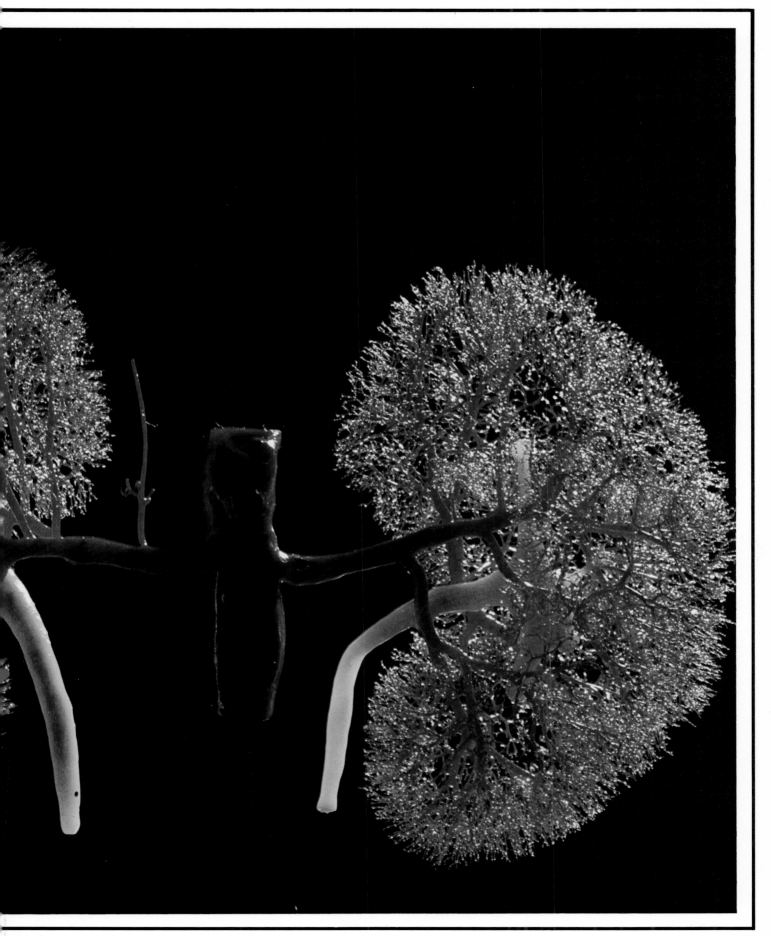

THE CELL

Cells are the basic-building blocks of the body. As a house is built from bricks, so our bodies are made from cells. Each of the 60 million or so cells in the body has its own special task, and cells come in all shapes and sizes. There are box-shaped cells, button-shaped cells, cells like giant balls, cells like tiny strands of wool, cells like tree-roots, even cells that look like tadpoles—all working in harmony to keep the body together.

Every cell is a hive of activity. To look at your skin, you might think that nothing much is going on. But inside each cell, there is a bustling chemical factory. Every second of the day, the cell's team of workers is busy ferrying chemicals to and fro, breaking up unwanted chemicals, making new ones, exploiting them on the spot or dispatching them to other cells, and much more.

What is more, few of these cells last very long. All the time, old cells are wearing out and new cells are created to replace them. Some cells last many months; others survive for less than a day. But every cell in the body—except the nerve cells—will hand over to a new cell sooner or later. In a way, the body is like a fountain, needing a constant flow of new water to keep its steady shape.

TEAM-WORK

Although there are many different kinds of cell within your body, they all stem from a single cell created by the fusion of a sperm cell from your father and an egg from your mother. This single cell divided and re-divided many millions of times to make your body. As it divided, in a process not fully understood, some of the new cells became skin cells and went to form the skin; others became nerve cells, muscle cells, fat cells and many more. But as the cells grew apart, they retained many of the same features. Although they have different shapes and functions, most cells are built up in the same way and have the same team of workers, working together to perform the cell's allotted task.

Living cells are squidgy cases containing a jelly-like mixture of chemicals called the protoplasm. They gain their rigidity by clumping

liver cell

fat cells

sperm cell

skin cell

nerve cell

muscle cell

nerve cell

bone cells

red blood cells

Many different kinds of cell go together to make up the body. The illustration above shows where some of the most important types can be found.

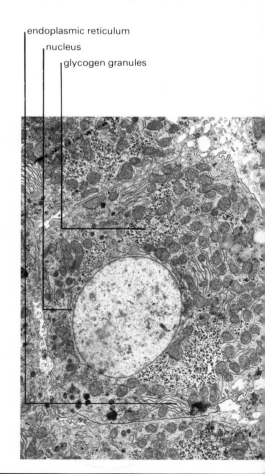

endoplasmic reticulum

nucleus

glycogen granules

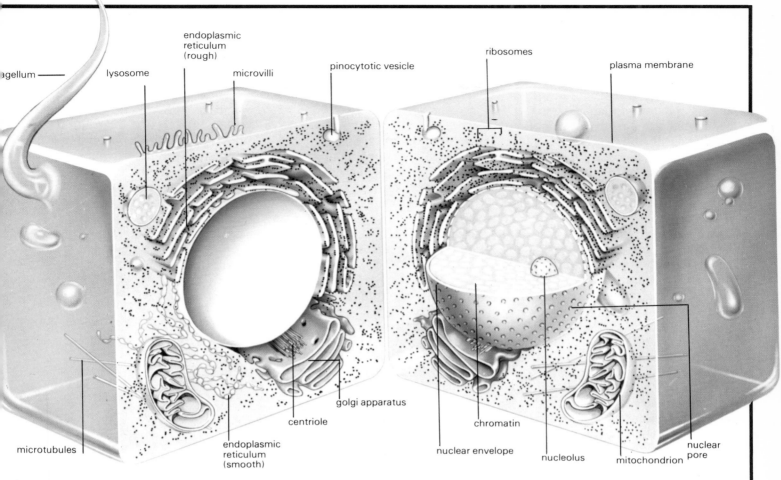

flagellum — lysosome — endoplasmic reticulum (rough) — microvilli — pinocytotic vesicle — ribosomes — plasma membrane — golgi apparatus — centriole — endoplasmic reticulum (smooth) — chromatin — nuclear envelope — nucleolus — mitochondrion — nuclear pore — microtubules

Above: The living cell is a dynamic, intricate chemical factory. Within the jelly of the cytoplasm are numerous specialized structures performing different tasks.

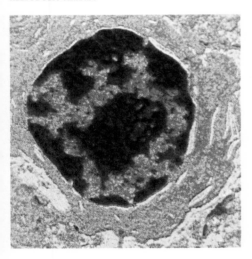

A microscope view of a cell in the liver, magnified 8000 times (left). The folds of endoplasmic reticulum and the numerous mitochondria (the small dark lumps) are clearly visible around the nucleus. Above is a kidney cell.

together. Holding the cell together is a thin carpet of fat, dotted with protein, called the membrane. Although the membrane holds the contents of the cell in place, it lets certain chemicals move in and out. The proteins, for instance, are very selective gateways for chemicals with small molecules, such as oxygen. Molecules too big to fit through the protein gates may still pass in and out of the cell by dissolving in the fatty cell membrane.

Inside the cell, there is a watery substance called the cytoplasm and floating in the cytoplasm is an inner cell called the nucleus. The nucleus is the control centre of the cell, containing the blueprints for all the cell's tasks. Every time the cell needs a new chemical, for instance, a messenger is sent from the nucleus with instructions.

Outside the nucleus in the cytoplasm, there is a complex mixture of dissolved chemicals and

particles washing around an intricate network of structures called organelles. Each of the organelles seems to have a particular function.

The sausage-shaped mitochondria are the power-houses of the cell. Between the internal partitions of the mitochondria chemical fuel supplied by the blood is used to charge up the cell's batteries by making a chemical called ATP (see page 44). The intricate network of flattened sacks called the Golgi complex is the export and packing centre of the cell. Here chemicals are stowed in minute membrane bags ready for dispatch to the cell and beyond. The ribosomes are places where protein, the raw material of body structures, is built up from chemicals called amino acids. And the lysosomes are the waste disposal units, breaking up unwanted material and retrieving useful parts.

BREATHING

If you have ever tried holding your breath, you will know if is impossible to keep up for long. Sooner or later you just have to breathe again. This is just as well, for if you did stop breathing altogether, you would soon lose consciousness and, in a matter of minutes, almost certainly die.

Breathing is, quite literally, vital. When we breathe in, we take air into the body. Without this frequent intake of air, every cell would rapidly break down. For air contains the oxygen needed to sustain the cell and fuel its various tasks. Just as a fire only burns if there is plenty of air, so each cell needs oxygen to burn up the food it receives from the blood and release the energy locked within. The process by which this occurs is called cellular respiration.

Food arrives at the cell in the form of a chemical called glucose, which is a kind of sugar (see pages 22-23). When glucose is burned in the cell

to release its store of energy, the hydrogen in it combines with oxygen to make water; the carbon also combines with oxygen to make carbon dioxide. Carbon dioxide is useless to the body and must be removed. This is what happens when we breathe out. The removal of carbon dioxide is as important as the intake of oxygen; if the body becomes clogged with carbon dioxide, we die just as surely as we would if we failed to breathe in oxygen.

Air enters the body via a pair of large greyish-pink bags in the chest called lungs. Like two squidgy foam-rubber cushions, the lungs encase an intricate network of tubes

that lead air to and from the mouth and nose. This network of airways is shaped rather like a hollow tree.

Every time we take a breath, air rushes swiftly through the pharynx and into the broad trunk of the tree called the larynx. Over the taut ligaments of the vocal cords it streams, and on down into the windpipe (the trachea), until it reaches a fork deep within the chest. At this fork, the airways branch into two, one branch or bronchus leading to the right lung, one to the left lung. Once in the lungs, the air flows gradually slower

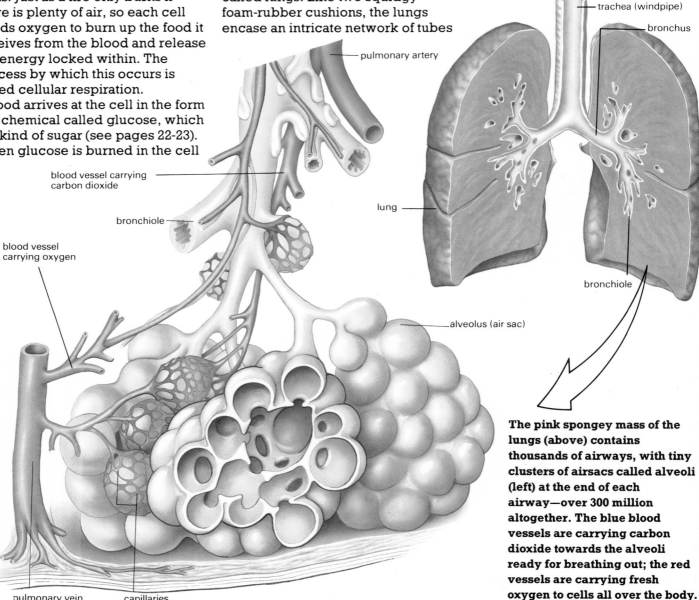

pulmonary artery

blood vessel carrying carbon dioxide

bronchiole

blood vessel carrying oxygen

trachea (windpipe)

bronchus

lung

bronchiole

alveolus (air sac)

pulmonary vein   capillaries

The pink spongey mass of the lungs (above) contains thousands of airways, with tiny clusters of airsacs called alveoli (left) at the end of each airway—over 300 million altogether. The blue blood vessels are carrying carbon dioxide towards the alveoli ready for breathing out; the red vessels are carrying fresh oxygen to cells all over the body.

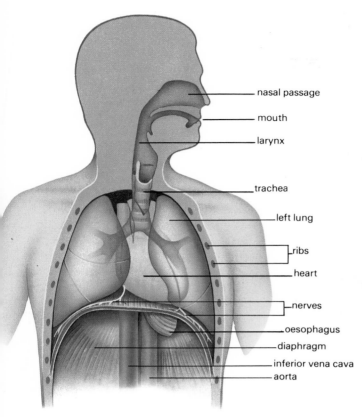

nasal passage
mouth
larynx
trachea
left lung
ribs
heart
nerves
oesophagus
diaphragm
inferior vena cava
aorta

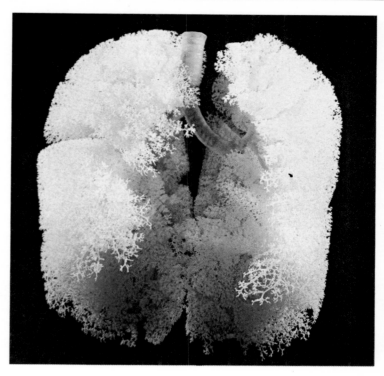

Left: The lungs are set in a cavity in the chest, supported by the rib cage and a sheet of muscle called the diaphragm. Above: A resin cast of the respiratory tree of the lungs.

and slower as the airways divide and re-divide, becoming narrower each time, until it finally reaches the tiny twig-like bronchioles.

Around the end of each bronchiole are clustered, like bunches of grapes, hundreds of minute round sacs called alveoli. The alveoli are the gateways for oxygen into the body. For oxygen is carried to each of the body's cells in the blood stream, and each alveolus is encircled by a network of tiny blood vessels—like a string bag around a football. Oxygen seeps through the thin walls of the alveoli and into the surrounding blood vessels. The blood, slowing down as it squeezes through the tiny blood vessels, picks up the oxygen and bears it away to cells all over the body. Carbon dioxide passes into the alveoli in the same way.

HOW THE LUNGS WORK

Air is rarely in the lungs for more than a few seconds, so this exchange must take place very quickly. This is where the tree-like

shape of the respiratory tract comes in. Its branching structure means there are over 2400 km (1500 miles) of airway. With such a large surface area, a great deal of oxygen can seep through, and an equal amount of carbon dioxide can seep back in a very short time, even though it only seeps through slowly at any one place.

On average, we breathe in and out roughly a litre of air every ten seconds, though the rate increases when we are working hard. Breathing out needs no effort, because the lungs are made of

spongey, elastic tissue and collapse like a balloon when air is exhaled—though they can only collapse so far because they are 'stuck' to the walls of the chest by a thin layer of pleural fluid. To breathe in, however, muscles must pull the chest outwards, expanding the lungs and drawing air in. This occurs as intercostal muscles between the ribs lift the ribcage up and outwards. At the same time, a domed sheet of muscle beneath the lungs, called the diaphragm, flattens out, pulling the lungs down and further expanding them.

Fact file . . .

We take about 600 million breaths during our lifetime.

Opened out and laid flat, the lungs would cover an area the size of a tennis court.

Every minute we breathe in about 6 l (10 pts) of air.

13

CIRCULATION

Once in the blood, oxygen must be delivered swiftly to the cells where it is needed. At the same time, the unwanted carbon dioxide must be collected from the cells and brought to the lungs for breathing out. This is where the body's remarkable system of blood circulation comes in.

Driven by a powerful pump (the heart), blood is piped throughout the body in an intricate network of blood vessels. As if on a roundabout with no exit, blood flows continually round and round the body, carrying oxygen and carbon dioxide between lungs and cells. Day and night throughout our lives, blood rich in oxygen streams away from our lungs bearing this vital gas to every part of the body. Day and night, the circulating blood gathers unwanted carbon dioxide from the cells and returns with it to the lungs.

TWO SYSTEMS

Blood circulation is actually split into two distinct systems—although the same blood runs through both—and there is a separate pump for each. Both systems start and finish at the heart, and the two pumps are simply the different sides of the heart. The smaller system feeds the lungs alone and is known as the pulmonary circulation. The larger, systemic circulation feeds the rest of the body.

SYSTEMIC FLOW

The systemic circulation begins in the strong left-hand side of the heart, which is supplied with oxygen-rich blood from the lungs. The left heart pumps this oxygen-rich blood away through large blood vessels called arteries. So thick are the walls of the arteries and so quickly does the blood flow that very little of the oxygen load can seep through to the tissues en route. All the way along the main arteries, however, there are many branches called arterioles which, in turn, branch into millions of tiny capillaries less than a hundredth of a millimetre thick.

As the blood is squeezed slowly through the capillaries, some of its load of oxygen seeps through the thin walls and into the fluid-filled space between the tissue cells. From here, individual cells can draw all the oxygen they need. At the same time, the blood moving through the capillaries picks up the unwanted carbon dioxide and carries it on into the network that returns blood to the heart.

The return network is like the outward network and in many places they run alongside each other. But the gradually widening blood vessels are not called arterioles and arteries but venules and veins. The two largest veins, the superior and inferior vena cava, return blood to the right-hand side of the heart. This blood is low in oxygen but high in carbon dioxide. So the right heart pumps the blood forward into the pulmonary system where the carbon dioxide can be exchanged for fresh oxygen in the lungs.

PULMONARY FLOW

The pulmonary is rather like a small version of the systemic. A broad artery takes blood away from the heart. This branches into smaller arterioles leading to each lung and eventually into capillaries wrapped around the alveoli (the air sacs). Here the oxygen supply is replenished and carbon dioxide removed. The blood is then fed back to the heart through a short network of veins ready to be pumped forward into the systemic.

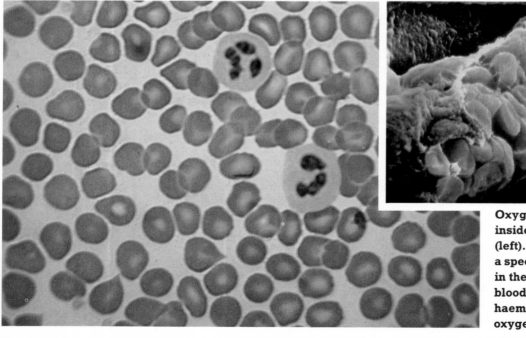

Oxygen is ferried through the blood inside button-shaped red blood cells (left). As blood washes over the lungs, a special molecule called haemoglobin in the red cells picks up oxygen. When blood reaches the capillaries, haemoglobin releases its cargo of oxygen to the cells (above).

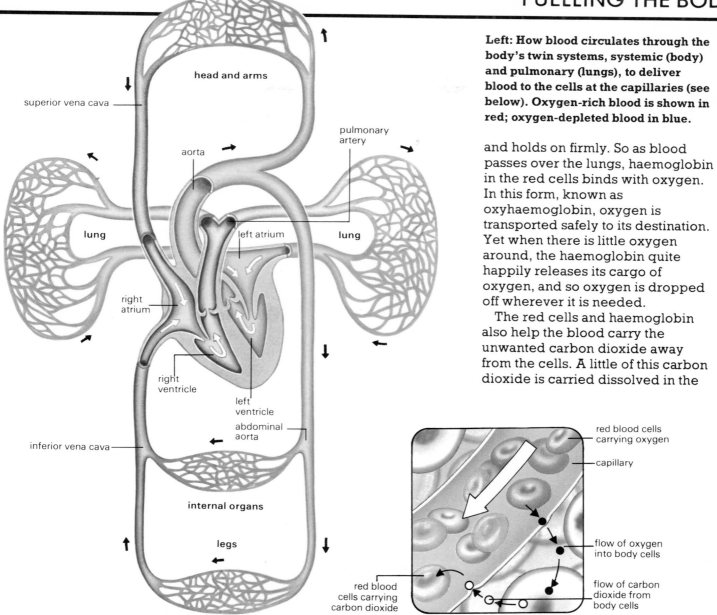

head and arms

superior vena cava

pulmonary artery

aorta

lung

left atrium

lung

right atrium

right ventricle

left ventricle

abdominal aorta

inferior vena cava

internal organs

legs

Left: How blood circulates through the body's twin systems, systemic (body) and pulmonary (lungs), to deliver blood to the cells at the capillaries (see below). Oxygen-rich blood is shown in red; oxygen-depleted blood in blue.

red blood cells carrying oxygen

capillary

flow of oxygen into body cells

flow of carbon dioxide from body cells

red blood cells carrying carbon dioxide

and holds on firmly. So as blood passes over the lungs, haemoglobin in the red cells binds with oxygen. In this form, known as oxyhaemoglobin, oxygen is transported safely to its destination. Yet when there is little oxygen around, the haemoglobin quite happily releases its cargo of oxygen, and so oxygen is dropped off wherever it is needed.

The red cells and haemoglobin also help the blood carry the unwanted carbon dioxide away from the cells. A little of this carbon dioxide is carried dissolved in the

It takes less than 90 seconds, on average, for blood to circulate—out from the left heart, round the body, back through the right heart and lungs to the left heart. The circulation time does vary considerably. It takes many minutes for the blood to travel to the feet and back, for instance; it takes only a matter of seconds to circulate around the coronary arteries serving the heart. But this 90 second average is remarkably quick when you realize that the average adult has more than 100,000 km (60,000 miles) of blood vessels and there are more than 60 billion cells throughout the body which must be supplied with blood.

OXYGEN RAFTS

Surprisingly, perhaps, oxygen is not just swept along by the blood. Instead, it is stowed safely inside tiny red, button-shaped cells called erythrocytes—which is simply Greek for red cell. There are hundreds of millions of these red cells, floating in the blood like rafts, ferrying oxygen through the body.

Each red cell can carry a great deal of oxygen because it contains a special substance called haemoglobin. Haemoglobin has a unique relationship with oxygen. When there is plenty of oxygen about, haemoglobin embraces it

blood without any help from the red cells. But most has to be dissolved inside the red cells before it can be carried in the blood. And some of the carbon dioxide is carried, like oxygen, by the haemoglobin inside the red cell.

When carrying oxygen, haemoglobin glows bright scarlet, and this is what makes blood red. But when the oxygen is released, haemoglobin fades to dull purple and the colour of the blood fades with it. So de-oxygenated blood on its way back to the lungs looks a deep purply red. Similarly if the body is ever deprived of oxygen this plum-coloured blood makes the skin look almost blue.

THE HEART

The heart is one of the body's marvels, on the move every second of our lives to keep the blood circulating. Even while we sleep, the heart goes on tirelessly pumping away, never stopping for a moment. Perhaps 70 times a minute—much more when we are running about—the heart's powerful muscles contract to send great jets of blood shooting through the arteries.

During our lives, the heart performs a staggering amount of work. If we live to the age of 75, it may beat more than 3000 million times and pump over 200 million litres (60 million gallons) of blood around the body—enough blood to cover New York's Central Park to a depth of 15 metres (50 ft). Not surprisingly, some people's hearts do fail eventually. But for most of us, our heart is something we never have to think about—a totally reliable, automatic pump.

The steady beat of the heart owes much to the unique muscle it is made from. Heart muscle is unlike any other muscle in the body. While most muscle has to be prodded into action by an electrical trigger, heart muscle works all by itself, contracting and relaxing rhythmically without any prompting. Even when removed from the body altogether, a heart goes on beating away as long as it has blood to pump. Press a hand against the middle of your chest and you should feel your heart pounding away steadily inside, suspended in its tough bag called the pericardium.

TWIN PUMPS

The heart is not just one pump but two, as we saw earlier, each pump forming a side of the heart. A thick, muscular wall called the septum keeps the two sides completely separate.

The left side is the pump that pushes oxygen-rich blood from the lungs all around the body. Because it must pump blood so far, the left heart is much the bigger and stronger of the two. The smaller right heart, in contrast, propels the returning blood, low in oxygen, only as far as the lungs—just a few millimetres away.

Each of the heart's twin pumps is essentially the same. Blood from the veins enters the heart from the top flooding into the atrium—the first of the two chambers in each side of the heart. 'Atrium' is the Latin for entrance hall, and the atrium is simply the lobby where blood waits before it is ushered into the second chamber—with a little squeeze from the muscles of the atrium wall. The second chamber—the ventricle—is the main pumping chamber. Its walls are much thicker and more muscular than those of the atrium. It is the powerful contraction of these muscular walls that squeezes the blood out and sends it shooting upwards into the arteries.

ONE-WAY TRAFFIC

Vital to the pump action of the heart is a set of valves which ensure that blood can flow only one way. There are four valves altogether, two in each side of the heart—a large valve between the atrium and the ventricle and a smaller valve at the exit from the ventricle into the arteries.

Both the smaller valves are called semi-lunar because their flaps resemble half-moons. The larger valves have different names in each side of the heart: the valve in the right heart is called the tricuspid because it has three cusps or flaps;

THE CARDIAC CYCLE

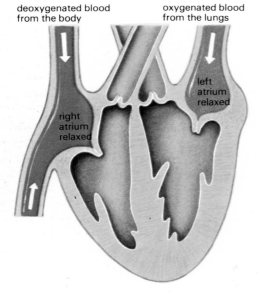

deoxygenated blood from the body

oxygenated blood from the lungs

right atrium relaxed

left atrium relaxed

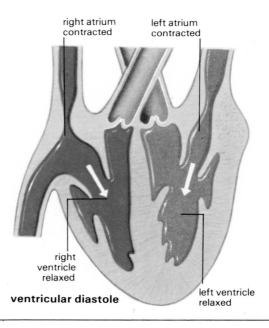

right atrium contracted

left atrium contracted

right ventricle relaxed

left ventricle relaxed

ventricular diastole

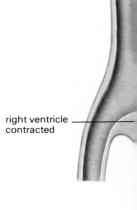

right ventricle contracted

The vital pump. This slice across the heart reveals its two V-shaped pumps clearly, although the larger left heart is partly hidden behind the right (as it is in the body).

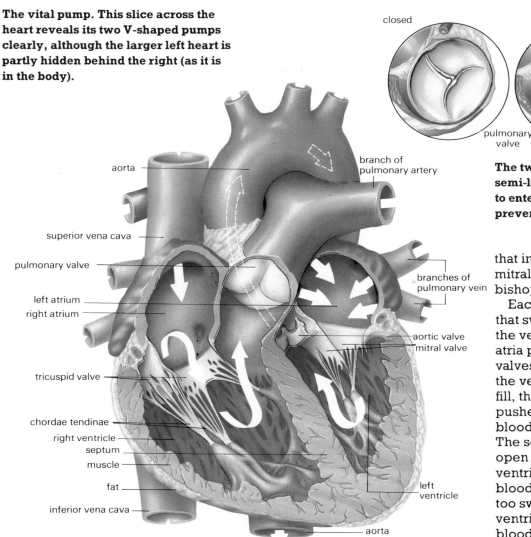

closed

open

pulmonary valve

The two details above show how the semi-lunar valve opens to allow blood to enter the arteries and shuts to prevent backflow.

aorta

branch of pulmonary artery

superior vena cava

pulmonary valve

branches of pulmonary vein

left atrium

right atrium

aortic valve

mitral valve

tricuspid valve

chordae tendinae

right ventricle

septum

muscle

fat

left ventricle

inferior vena cava

aorta

that in the left heart is known as the mitral because it looks a little like a bishop's mitre.

Each of these valves are trapdoors that swing open only one way. As the ventricles empty, blood in the atria pushes the mitral and tricuspid valves open and flows through into the ventricles. But as the ventricles fill, the pressure of blood gradually pushes these valves shut and stops blood running back into the atria. The semi-lunar valves are forced open when the walls of the ventricles contract and squeeze the blood out into the arteries. But they too swing shut as soon as the ventricles stop squeezing and blood tries to run back in.

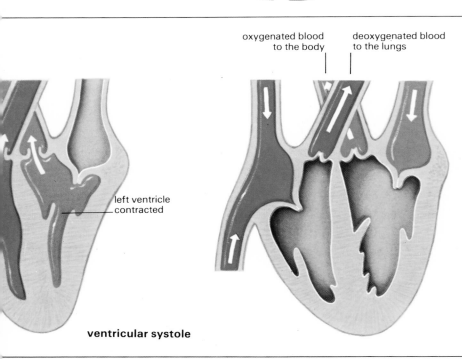

oxygenated blood to the body

deoxygenated blood to the lungs

left ventricle contracted

ventricular systole

Every time the heart beats (roughly every 0.8 seconds), it goes through the same sequence of events, called the cardiac cycle. The cycle has two main phases: systole (contraction) and diastole (relaxation). It begins as a wave of muscle contraction sweeps across the atria from right to left, pushing blood into the relaxed ventricles. This is called ventricular diastole. Less than a tenth of a second later, the wave reaches the ventricles and they too contract, squeezing blood up into the arteries (ventricular systole). After little more than half a second, both atria and ventricles relax again and the atria fill with blood. In under a second, the cycle is complete.

BLOOD FLOW

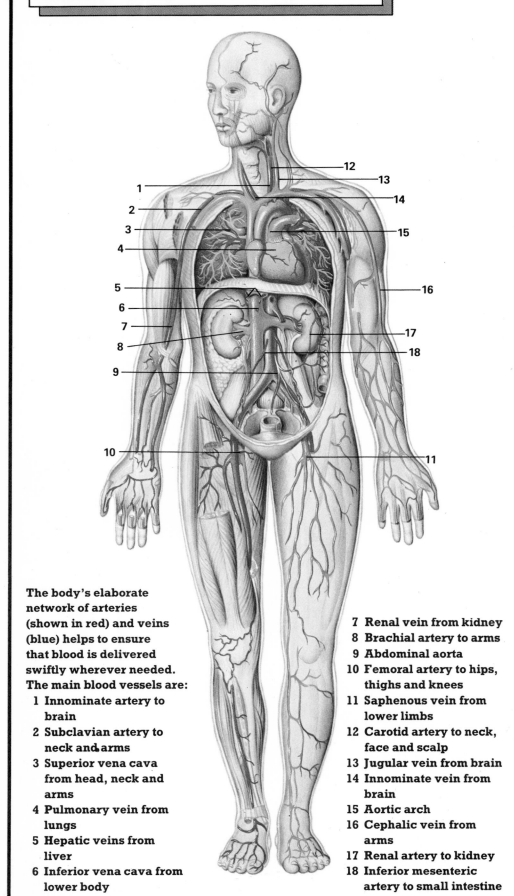

The body's elaborate
network of arteries
(shown in red) and veins
(blue) helps to ensure
that blood is delivered
swiftly wherever needed.
The main blood vessels are:
1 Innominate artery to
  brain
2 Subclavian artery to
  neck and arms
3 Superior vena cava
  from head, neck and
  arms
4 Pulmonary vein from
  lungs
5 Hepatic veins from
  liver
6 Inferior vena cava from
  lower body

7 Renal vein from kidney
8 Brachial artery to arms
9 Abdominal aorta
10 Femoral artery to hips,
   thighs and knees
11 Saphenous vein from
   lower limbs
12 Carotid artery to neck,
   face and scalp
13 Jugular vein from brain
14 Innominate vein from
   brain
15 Aortic arch
16 Cephalic vein from
   arms
17 Renal artery to kidney
18 Inferior mesenteric
   artery to small intestine

Much of the time, you would
hardly know your heart is there.
Yet there are always faint signs of
its tireless activity all over the
body. For, as the ventricles snap
rythmically in and out, they send
little tremors racing through the
blood. You can sometimes feel
these minute shock waves by
lightly touching the skin
wherever an artery comes near
the surface. This steady stream of
shock waves from the heart is
called the pulse.

The best place to feel the pulse
is on the inside of the wrist,
where the radial artery comes
near the surface. If you gently lay
the tips of your fingers over the
artery, you can feel the echo of
your heartbeat. By counting the
number of pulses per minute you
can tell exactly how fast your
heart is beating.

BLOOD ON DEMAND

The heart does not always beat at
the same rate. Sometimes it will
beat rapidly—perhaps 200 times in a
minute; sometimes it will beat
slowly. Guided by a constant
stream of messages from the brain,
the heart speeds up or slows down
to meet the body's ever-changing
need for oxygen. When beating
fast, the heart pumps more blood
and so boosts the oxygen supply;
when beating slowly, it pumps less
blood and the oxygen supply
drops. It beats fastest when the
body is working hard—running or
jumping, for instance—for hard
work makes muscle cells hungry
for oxygen as they burn extra fuel. It
beats slowest when we are resting.

In fact, the body's blood supply
has all kinds of checks and
balances to ensure each and every
cell gets just as much oxygen as it
needs. Blood vessels, for instance,
are not just passive pipes to channel
the flow; they have muscles and
valves to actively control the way
blood flows. Only the capillaries
exert no control at all.

One important task of the walls of
the arteries is to smooth the flow of

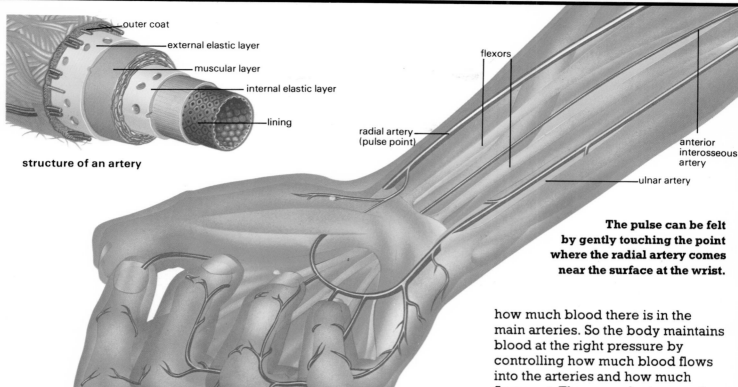

structure of an artery

- outer coat
- external elastic layer
- muscular layer
- internal elastic layer
- lining

flexors

radial artery
(pulse point)

anterior
interosseous
artery

ulnar artery

**The pulse can be felt
by gently touching the point
where the radial artery comes
near the surface at the wrist.**

blood. The heart pumps blood in a series of separate squirts. Yet blood flows through the body in a steady stream—only the pulse remains to recall the heart's pumping action. This is because the artery walls are elastic. When the heart squirts blood into the aorta, the aorta walls balloon out. So while some blood shoots straight down the arteries, some is delayed in the stretched aorta. But when each spurt from the heart is over, the walls of the aorta spring back, propelling this blood towards the smaller arteries.

In fact, a wave of stretching and recoil runs all the way along the artery walls with each surge of blood, getting smaller and smaller farther away from the heart.

MUSCULAR TAPS

The smaller arteries are less elastic but more muscular and they play an even more positive role in regulating blood flow. Their muscular walls are like taps that turn the blood flow on and off. Responding to a variety of signals,

these taps open and close to divert blood to the places where it is most needed. They open to increase the blood supply to active tissues and close to reduce it to resting tissues.

The muscular taps on the arterioles also play a vital part in the control of blood pressure. Like a town's water supply, blood in the main arteries must be at the right pressure—too little pressure and the oxygen in the blood may not reach the cells; too much and both cells and the arteries themselves may be damaged irreparably.

Blood pressure depends on

how much blood there is in the main arteries. So the body maintains blood at the right pressure by controlling how much blood flows into the arteries and how much flows out. The muscular taps on the arterioles adjust the flow of blood out of the main arteries; the flow into the arteries depends on the heart. If the heart beats powerfully and strongly, pressure in the arteries builds up; if it beats slowly and weakly, pressure is low.

Unlike your heart rate, blood pressure tends to remain relatively steady all the time. Scientists are not sure exactly how blood pressure is controlled. The nervous system plays a part. So does a substance released by the kidneys called renin. But no-one yet knows why some people have high blood pressure all the time—a condition called hypertension—and others do not.

Fact file . . .

Blood races through the arteries at up to 1 metre (3 ft) per second.

There are over 60,000 km (37,000 miles) of capillary in the body.

The average pulse rate is 80 per minute.

WHAT IS BLOOD?

If you have ever cut yourself and bled freely, you may have decided that blood is a nice colour but not very interesting—rather like red ink. Yet through a powerful microscope, you could see that blood has a rich and varied population of different cells, swept along in the clear, yellowish fluid called plasma. Even in the plasma itself are dissolved hundreds of different substances.

The blood is the body's transport system. It not only carries the vital oxygen supply to every single cell in the body, it also carries all the food needed to fuel and maintain the body's tissues—muscles, organs, skin, brain. It bears the chemical regulators that ensure each cell works as it should. It washes away all the unwanted material to liver, kidney and lungs. And it spreads heat evenly over the body to keep it at just the right temperature. What is more, blood plays a vital role in the body's defences against disease. With so many and varied tasks to perform, it is hardly surprising that it is such a complex liquid.

BLOOD CELLS

Blood cells fall into three main groups. By far the most numerous are the button-shaped red blood cells that carry oxygen (see pages 14-15). Then there are the tiny irregular platelets. And finally the giant white cells called leucocytes. Together, these cells make up just under half the volume of blood; the rest is plasma.

Unlike red cells, white cells do not act as rafts—although there are some white cells whose function

Blood contains an enormous number of different cells and chemicals, each performing its own vital role. In the test tube diagram on the right, the main constituents are shown in roughly the same proportions as they occur in the blood. The blood cells are shown in red; plasma fluids in blue.

Above: Blood transfusion—the removal of blood from, and injection of it into, the circulatory system—has been practised since the seventeenth century.

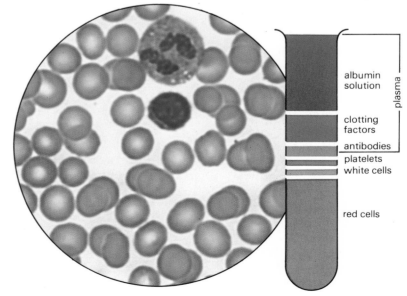

albumin solution

plasma

clotting factors

antibodies

platelets

white cells

red cells

cannot be identified. Instead, they are the key to the body's defences against invaders.

Most of the white blood cells are filled with tiny grains and so are called granular leucocytes. The most numerous of the granular leucocytes, called neutrophils, are scavengers. When they arrive at the site of an infection, they simply swallow any intruders and digest them. This process is called phagocytosis, which simply means cell eating.

The remaining two kinds of granular leucocyte, called eosinophils and basophils, are rather more mysterious. They are far less numerous—there are over 20 neutrophils to every eosinophil

and over 150 to every basophil. And their exact function is unclear. It seems likely that they, just as the neutrophils, take part in the fight against invaders. The basophils, for instance, are known to store a chemical called histamine which helps rush the blood's army of defenders to any site of infection.

Defence against invaders also seems to be the role of the white cells with grain-free interiors, the non-granular leucocytes. The monocytes are, like the neutrophils, scavenger cells that roam through the blood eating up debris and unwelcome guests. But they are real professionals, capable of disposing not only of the more obvious intruders but also, acting on instructions, of the more discreet foreign bodies.

The lymphocytes, the other main kind of non-granular white cell, are again part of the body's elaborate

defence mechanism. Their role is not simply cell eating, but something more complex. One of their tasks, for instance, is to help provide the instructions for the monocytes and other defence cells to identify intruders. Some lymphocytes, though, act as killer cells, attacking intruders directly.

BLOOD CLOTTING

The platelets look a little like tiny chips and, indeed, that is what they are; they are simply fragments that have broken from other cells during formation. Yet they too have an important role in the defence of the body. But rather than repelling intruders like the white cells, they prevent loss of blood by helping to plug any leak—such as a cut. They also help to prevent blood loss by releasing special clotting activators which help encourage the formation of fibres around the wound. Blood cells get caught up in the tangle of fibres and form a clot that plugs the leak.

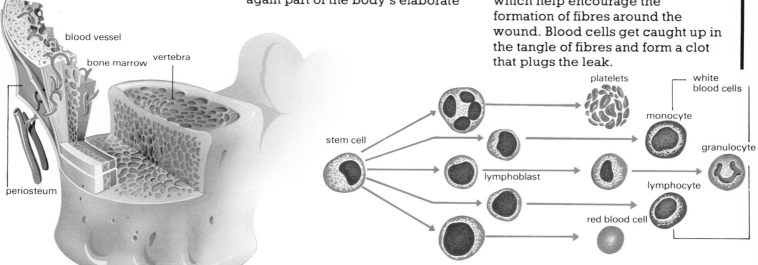

Few of the blood's cells live very long. Red cells die after four months; neutrophils survive little more than six hours. So the blood must be constantly topped up with new cells to replace those whose time is up. Nearly all these new cells are born, not in the blood, but in the soft red honeycomb called the marrow in the middle of certain bones—notably the spine, ribs and breastbone. Within the marrow, it is thought, a single type of cell called a stem cell divides progressively to form all the different types of blood cell.

Fact file . . .

There are 5 million red cells in every cubic millimetre of blood (80,000 million in a cubic inch).

1½ million red cells and over one million neutrophils are produced every second.

FOOD AND ENERGY

Like an engine, your body must have a constant supply of energy to keep it going. You need energy to run, to walk, work and play—you even need energy to sleep, for internal processes are as reliant on energy as muscular movements.

Energy needs vary from person to person, and different tasks require different amounts of energy. You need much more energy when your body is working hard than you do sitting quietly.

Besides the energy you need to move, you need a certain amount of energy just to keep basic bodily processes ticking over—to keep the heart beating and the lungs breathing, for instance. This is usually called the resting metabolism—metabolism is the way the body uses energy for its complex chemical processes.

Resting metabolism varies tremendously from person to person. Clearly, the bigger you are, the more energy you burn. But energy needs depend on the area of the body surface rather than weight. Surface area influences how much body heat is lost through the skin and how much energy you need to keep warm. So tall, thin people tend to have higher metabolic rates than shorter but fatter people of the same weight.

Our resting metabolic rate is not fixed, however, but varies throughout our lives. As you get older and stop growing, for instance, you need less and less energy. Similarly, the body adapts to different situations. Energy needs drop in tropical countries, for instance, because the body uses less energy to keep warm. But they also drop when the body is deprived of food. Body processes slow down and tick over using the bare minimum of energy to tide it over the famine period. This is why slimming diets are often difficult to make effective. As a man eats less, his body burns food more and more slowly to eke it out. Metabolic rate also varies with lifestyle. Athletes, for instance, seem to burn up more energy than the average person even when they are sitting still.

FOOD ENERGY

All the energy we need to fuel body processes comes from eating food. Food contains energy for the body in three main forms: carbohydrates, fats and protein.

The body uses carbohydrates, fats and proteins in many different ways. Carbohydrates are the main source of energy; fats are stored energy; and protein is used as a building material for all the tissues and cells of the body.

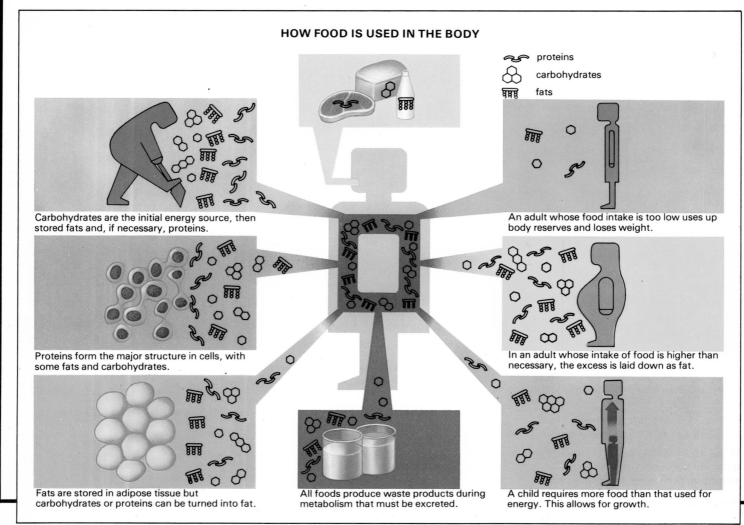

HOW FOOD IS USED IN THE BODY

~~ proteins
⬡ carbohydrates
≣ fats

Carbohydrates are the initial energy source, then stored fats and, if necessary, proteins.

Proteins form the major structure in cells, with some fats and carbohydrates.

Fats are stored in adipose tissue but carbohydrates or proteins can be turned into fat.

All foods produce waste products during metabolism that must be excreted.

An adult whose food intake is too low uses up body reserves and loses weight.

In an adult whose intake of food is higher than necessary, the excess is laid down as fat.

A child requires more food than that used for energy. This allows for growth.

sucrose molecule

oxygen
hydrogen
carbon

Left: Sugar in the sugar bowl is just one of the half a dozen types of sugar found in food. Its complex sucrose molecule must be broken down into glucose before it can be used as a body fuel.

Carbohydrates are by far the most important source of day-to-day energy for most people. Weight for weight, fat is actually twice as rich in energy, but the energy in carbohydrates is easier for the body to use. Indeed, the brain can only use a certain type of carbohydrate called glucose.

There are two main types of carbohydrate: starch and sugar. Nearly all cereals and root vegetables contain some starch. Bread and rice are particularly heavy in starch. Sugars come in many different shapes. Besides the sugar in the sugar bowl, which is mainly a sugar called sucrose, there are a variety of sugars in different foods. Many fruit, for instance, contain a sugar called fructose. Maltose comes from barley and lactose from milk. To use all these carbohydrates, the body breaks them down in the digestive tract to a simple sugar called glucose. This can be used directly to fuel the cells or temporarily stored in the liver and muscles as glycogen.

Fats are energy-rich, which makes them an ideal way of storing energy in the body. They are less weight to carry around than carbohydrates for the amount of energy they hold. So the body distributes fats to various parts of the body, ready to call on in times of need. Nevertheless, in more affluent parts of the world, fats provide 40 per cent of all the body's energy needs. Like carbohydrates, they come in many forms and are found in many foods. Butter and dairy products contain especially high proportions of fat.

Protein is the last, and least used, of the three energy sources. Protein has many other uses in the body and is only used as an energy source in emergencies.

ENERGY EXPENDITURE WITH VARIOUS ACTIVITIES

walking up stairs — 900 (3780)
skiing — 800 (3360)
— 700 (2940)
— 600 (2520)
swimming —
dancing — 500 (2100)
cycling — 400 (1680)
gardening — 300 (1260)
sweeping — 200 (840)
walking slowly — 100 (420)
sitting / standing
lying down — 0

kilocalories expended per hour (kJ/h)

Although we use some energy even when we are asleep, muscles burn up energy at an enormous rate, and vigorous exercise pushes up the rate of energy consumption by over ten times above the resting metabolic rate.

A HEALTHY DIET

Most of the food we eat is used by the body for energy. Sugars, starches, fats and even proteins go into the ever-hungry furnace of cell metabolism. We have little trouble in telling when we need more food for energy; hunger is our body's way of telling us we do.

In Europe and North America, where there is abundant food, it is very easy to eat more energy-rich food than your body needs. As a result, many more people are overweight in these countries than anywhere else in the world. A large intake of fat, mainly dairy products and meat, is perhaps the main cause.

Scientists are still not certain precisely what weight people should be and the ideal weight for one person is not the ideal weight for another. But it is clear that excess weight can be bad for health. There is a definite link between excess weight and heart problems, for instance. There is also considerable pressure from society to stay slim. So a good balance between the energy your body needs and the energy your body gets in the food you eat is clearly important.

VITAL EXTRAS

For good health, our diet must include small quantities of other materials besides energy food. Unfortunately, the body is not so good at indicating when it needs these materials as it is at calling for energy. Often, we only know that something has been missing from our diet when the body begins to go wrong. This is why it is important to monitor your diet carefully.

Protein is particularly important. Although it is rarely used by the body as a fuel, protein plays a vital role in the structure of the body. Protein is the main building material in cells and body tissues. So a constant supply of protein is essential for all new growth and repairing damaged or worn out

VITAMIN	FUNCTIONS FACILITATED	GOOD SOURCES
A—retinol	Regulates growth and differentiation of glandular ducts and epithelial cells; needed for rapidly growing or regenerating surfaces such as eyes and lungs; may help prevent growth of tumours.	Liver, fish, dairy produce, eggs, carrots, gre vegetables (particularly spinach), margarine
B₁—thiamine	Pain inhibitor; essential for digestion, growth and muscle tone; required for release of energy from carbohydrates.	Most carbohydrate-rich food such as bread, flour and potatoes; meat, milk, peas, beans, brewer's yeast, wheatgerm.
B₂—riboflavin	Necessary for converting food to energy.	Milk, organ meat (particularly liver), eggs, green vegetables.
B₆—pyridoxine	Involved in metabolism of amino acids, including conversion of tryptophan to nicotinic acid; necessary for formation of haemoglobin in red blood cells; may have anti-thrombotic properties.	Most foods—particularly liver, yeast, cereals, bread, milk products, eggs.
B₁₂—cyanocobal-amin	Needed by rapidly dividing cells such as those in bone marrow which form blood; contributes to healthy nervous system and normal growth.	Dairy and animal products (particularly liver) can be synthesized by bacteria in the gut.
Biotin	Part of several enzyme systems, it facilitates cell growth, fatty acid production and metabolism.	Egg yolk, liver, kidney, yeast and most foods; made by bacteria in the gut.
Folic acid	Needed by rapidly dividing cells such as those in bone marrow, which form blood; claimed to help prevent neural tube defects such as spina bifida if taken early in or prior to pregnancy.	Most green leafy vegetables, offal, pulses, bread, oranges, bananas.
Nicotinic acid—niacin	Necessary for converting food to energy; aids nervous system; needed for maintaining appetite and healthy skin.	Lean meat, enriched cereals and bread, eggs, milk products.
Panthothenic acid	Needed for growth stimulation, antibody production, metabolism of fat and carbohydrates.	Nearly all foods.
C—ascorbic acid	Essential for maintaining healthy teeth, gums and bones; may have role in synthesizing and breaking down cholesterol, fighting infection and modifying the body's response to potentially toxic substances—particularly cancer-causing nitrosamines commonly found in food and water.	Fresh fruit (particularly citrus and black currants), green vegetables, potatoes.
D—calciferol (a hormone, not a vitamin)	Necessary for maintaining levels of calcium and phosphorous in the blood and transporting calcium to and from bones.	Cod liver oil, egg yolk, salmon, tuna, butter; most important source is sunlight.
E—tocopherol	Antioxidant in the blood which helps keep the membranes of red blood cells healthy; prevents retrolental fibroplasia (blindness in premature babies).	Vegetable oils, wheatgerm, eggs, nuts, fruit green vegetables.
K—phylloquinone	Necessary for normal blood clotting.	Green vegetables, oatmeal, liver; made by bacteria in the gut.

tissue. The body does not use protein from food directly. Instead the food proteins are broken down into amino acids by the digestion. The cells then make their own proteins using these amino acids as building blocks.

Protein is found in an enormous variety of foods and so very few people in affluent countries suffer from protein deficiency. But there are two kinds of protein. The protein in meat is called first class protein because it contains all the amino acids the body needs. No one plant contains all these acids, so plant protein is called second class protein. Vegetarians can ensure they take in all the right amino acids by eating a variety of food plants.

Besides protein, the body also

needs minute traces of chemicals that it cannot make for itself: vitamins and minerals. Vitamins are needed to help drive some of the processes in the cell. When they were first discovered, they were given letter names, such as Vitamin D. Later on, however, newly-discovered vitamins were given chemical names. So there is an odd mixture of the two. Vitamins are found in an enormous variety of foods and used for an equally large range of tasks around the body. The table opposite shows just some of these functions.

Essential minerals include small quantities of salt, calcium for bones, iron for red blood cells and a few others in minute quantities—iodine, for example.

Besides carbohydrates, fats and proteins, the body must have small quantities of certain vitamins (left). Some stay in the body for months, so there is no need to eat these in every meal; a balanced diet including liver, milk, and fresh green vegetables should provide all the vitamins needed.

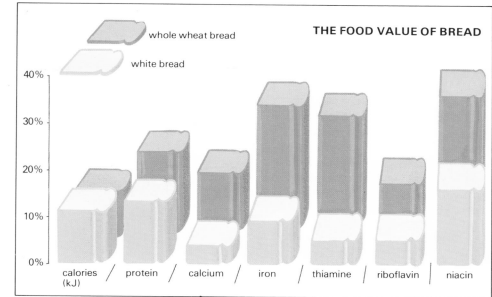

THE FOOD VALUE OF BREAD

whole wheat bread

white bread

calories (kJ) / protein / calcium / iron / thiamine / riboflavin / niacin

WHERE FOOD GOES

Each of the body's cells is supplied with food in the form of small, simple molecules, carried in the blood. Yet the food we eat comes in solid lumps and liquids made up from large, complex molecules. So the body has developed an elaborate chain of mechanisms to break down the food we eat into molecules that can be carried by the blood and absorbed into the cells.

The process of breakdown starts as soon as you put food in your mouth. The jaw muscles are enormously powerful—for their size, perhaps the most powerful in the body—and they grind the teeth together with such force that food is soon chewed to a pulp.

When the food is ready to be swallowed, the tongue thrusts the lump of food, or bolus, back towards the throat. The palate rises to block off the passages to the nose, and the entrance to the larynx is drawn shut. The bolus is then squeezed down into the oesophagus, the tube that leads to the stomach.

THE GUT

Once in the oesophagus, food begins its long and arduous journey through the alimentary canal or gut tube. As it travels through the canal, the food is assaulted by a battery of muscular and chemical agents, each designed to break it down further towards the simple molecules needed by the cells, a process called digestion.

The alimentary canal is very long—almost 10 metres (30 ft)—and is folded over and over in the abdomen like a pile of rope. Food takes 24 hours or more to pass right the way through. But the canal is not just a long tube; it is an elaborate chain of organs, each with its own part to play in the breakdown of food.

The main organs of the digestive system are folded tightly within the abdomen. All have muscular walls that help move food through the gut.

Not even the oesophagus is simply an inert tube. Its walls contain powerful muscles arranged both in rings around the tube and in bands along it. Whenever a bolus of food enters the oesophagus, rings of muscle just above the bolus contract sharply while those below relax. So the bolus is squeezed down the tube. Waves of muscle contraction and relaxation pulse down the gut tube, pushing the bolus further and further towards the stomach. This process is called peristalsis and plays a vital part in the movement of food through all

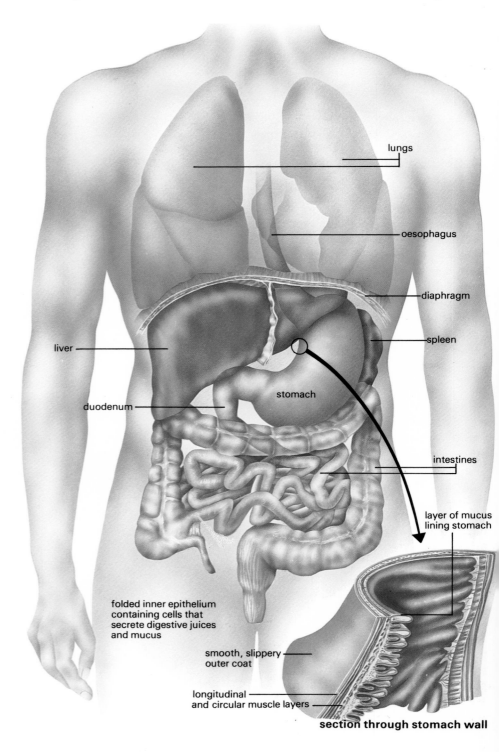

lungs

oesophagus

diaphragm

spleen

liver

stomach

duodenum

intestines

layer of mucus lining stomach

folded inner epithelium containing cells that secrete digestive juices and mucus

smooth, slippery outer coat

longitudinal and circular muscle layers

section through stomach wall

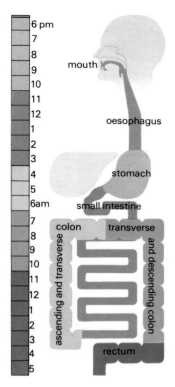

Above: Food takes on average 24 hours to pass through the alimentary canal.

Right: Food is moved through the gut by waves of peristalsis, with muscles contracting behind the bolus of chyme and relaxing in front.

parts of the gut, not just the oesophagus. But peristalsis not only helps to move food, it also mixes and batters the food ready for chemical assault.

DIGESTION

It is in the bag-like stomach that the process of digestion begins in earnest. The walls of the stomach are very strong and, as the stomach begins to fill, waves of peristaltic contraction spread across it every 20 seconds or so, pounding and churning the food within. At the same time, glands in the stomach wall secrete gastric juices—acids and enzymes—that start to dissolve the food chemically. To protect the stomach from its own juices, the walls are lined with a thick layer of mucus—though occasionally this breaks down, causing a painful stomach ulcer.

Besides setting the breakdown of food in motion, the stomach acts as a store for the partially-digested food, letting it through gradually into the next stage of the canal, the small intestine. When empty, the stomach is small, with a capacity of half a litre (less than a pint). But after a heavy meal it may stretch to hold two litres (3½ pts) or more.

The stomach is separated from the small intestine by a ring of thick muscle called the pyloric sphincter. The pyloric sphincter, like other sphincters in the gut, acts like a rubber band around the opening of a bag. As it tightens or relaxes, it controls the amount of food that can pass through.

When the pyloric sphincter relaxes and lets food through into the small intestine, it is in a semi-fluid mass called chyme. Over the great length of the small intestine—over 7 metres (more than 20 ft)—the chyme is broken down further still into the simple molecules that can be absorbed into the bloodstream and carried to the cells. Most of the digestion takes place in a section of the small intestine called the duodenum while most food is absorbed, or ingested, into the bloodstream in the ileum. Food that cannot be digested passes on into the large intestine and is then expelled from the body through the anus.

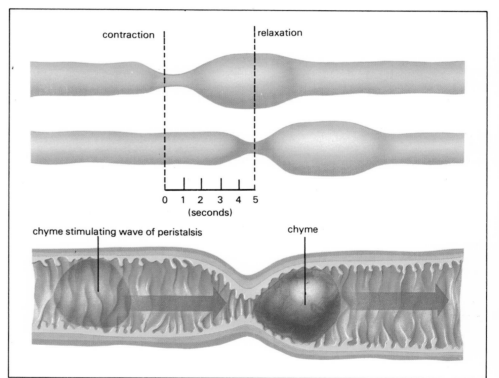

Fact file . . .

The stomach is situated not at the navel as you may think but just below and to the left of the breastbone.

The gut is six times as long as you are tall.

Even thought of food can start the gastric juices flowing.

DIGESTION

For hours after every meal, the alimentary canal buzzes with activity. The canal is the body's food refinery, and it works non-stop to break down the food we eat into the pure and simple elements the body needs.

The chemical attack begins almost the moment we lay eyes on food. The mere sight of a juicy steak or a cream cake can be enough to set the mouth watering as saliva oozes from glands around the mouth. Saliva not only helps to lubricate food so that it slips more easily down the throat; it also contains an enzyme called amylase which is the first of the body's chemical weapons, and lies ready in wait for food in the mouth.

Enzymes are special chemicals that prod all kinds of body processes into action. The digestive process relies on a wide range of such chemicals, each assisting in the breakdown of a specific part of the food. Digestive enzymes do not actually break up the food themselves; they simply get the processes going. But the results are the same and the digestive enzymes can be thought of as biological scissors, snipping away at the giant food molecules, like kitchen scissors on a string of sausages.

SPLITTING SUGARS

The amylase in the mouth works on starchy molecules—found in bread, fruit and vegetables, for example—chopping them into simpler sugars. But its role in digestion is small, for it is neutralized as soon as it reaches the stomach with the food. Like all enzymes, it is very sensitive to its working conditions and it will not work in the acid environment of the stomach. Similarly many other

Right: Tiny finger-like villi give a huge surface in the intestine for absorbing food.

digestive enzymes will only perform their tasks when they meet the right chemical triggers.

The breakdown of carbohydrates into simple sugars only begins again once the stomach acids have themselves been neutralized in the duodenum. There, another version of amylase continues the process started in the mouth. This enzyme, like a number of other vital digestive enzymes, comes through a thin tube from a long, spongey organ called the pancreas.

Below: Greenish bile from the gall bladder works like washing-up liquid to break up, or emulsify, large globules of fat.

Soon the carbohydrates are cut down into simple sugars—such as maltose, sucrose and lactose. But even these are too big for ready absorption into the bloodstream, so another set of enzymes gets to work as the food moves on down through the intestine. Each of these new enzymes has its own target: maltase splits up maltose molecules; sucrase splits sucrose molecules; lactase lactose molecules.

At last, all the vulnerable carbohydrates are split into glucose and other molecules, tiny enough to slip through the walls of the gut and into the bloodstream. Those carbohydrates that have resisted attack, such as cellulose, pass on into the large intestine and, from there, out of the body.

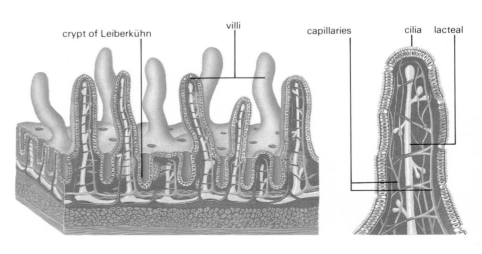

crypt of Leiberkühn   villi   capillaries   cilia   lacteal

Above: The tiny villi that are vital to food absorption can only be seen under a microscope.

PROTEINS AND FATS

Proteins are broken down in much the same way, but the process begins in the stomach. Some glands in the stomach wall secrete acid and some an enzyme called pepsinogen. By itself, pepsinogen has no effect, but when it meets the acid inside the stomach, it becomes pepsin, a potent protein chopper. Pepsin quickly snips the protein in food into short chains of amino acids—fortunately, the body's own protein in the stomach walls is protected by the thick layer of mucus. The amino acid chains are broken down even further in the small intestine, first by trypsin and then by a variety of enzymes called peptidases, Eventually, only single amino acids are left.

Fats are also broken down in the small intestine, by an enzyme called lipase. But before lipase can get to work, the ground must be prepared by a remarkable greenish fluid called bile which comes, via the gall bladder, from the liver. Bile acts like washing-up liquid to break up large globules of fat into tiny droplets vulnerable to lipase.

By the time the slimy chyme of food reaches the last part of the small intestine, the ileum, digestion is as complete as it will ever be. The next stage is the ingestion of the simple food molecules into the bloodstream. As we shall see, millions of tiny projections called villi in the lining of the ileum play a major role in this process.

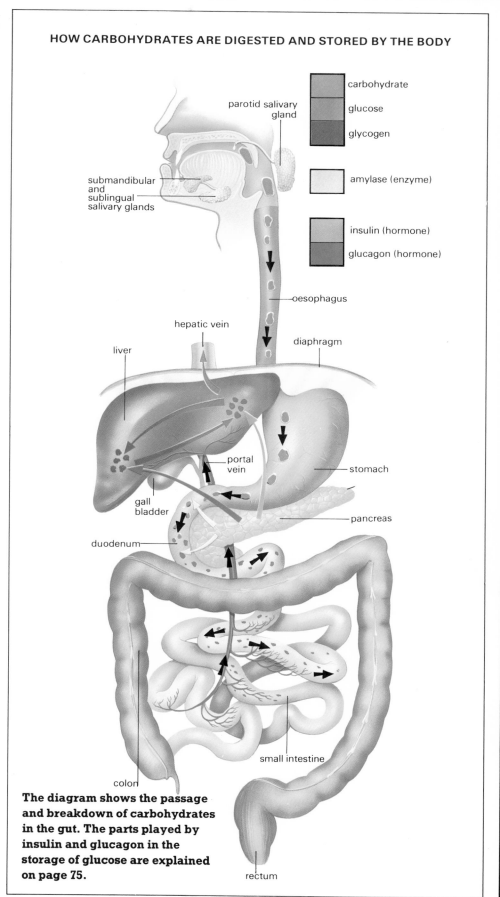

HOW CARBOHYDRATES ARE DIGESTED AND STORED BY THE BODY

- carbohydrate
- glucose
- glycogen
- amylase (enzyme)
- insulin (hormone)
- glucagon (hormone)

parotid salivary gland

submandibular and sublingual salivary glands

oesophagus

hepatic vein

liver

diaphragm

portal vein

stomach

gall bladder

pancreas

duodenum

small intestine

colon

rectum

The diagram shows the passage and breakdown of carbohydrates in the gut. The parts played by insulin and glucagon in the storage of glucose are explained on page 75.

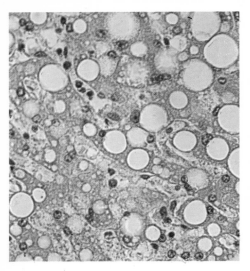

Above: Eating too many fatty foods can cause fat droplets like these to accumulate in the liver.

Just like oxygen, digested food is carried to all the cells of the body in the bloodstream. And just as oxygen gets into the blood by seeping through the walls of the lungs, so food enters by seeping through the walls of the gut.

The small intestine owes its vast surface area not only to its great length, but also to the millions of folds upon folds in the gut wall. For upon the back of each large pleat are microscopic finger-like folds called villi; and upon each villus are even tinier folds called microvilli. Again, just as alveoli are covered in myriad tiny blood vessels that carry oxygen away from the lungs, so hundreds of capillaries are packed into each villus to bear food swiftly away from the gut.

The gut can go on supplying food for many hours as food moving down the tube is gradually broken down. Indeed, the gut is often still absorbing food from one meal when you eat the next. This means there is food entering the bloodstream nearly all the time.

Once absorbed, food is swept by the blood through the capillaries into veins running around the gut, and finally into the giant portal vien. This vein channels the food-laden blood right into the liver.

THE LIVER

Of all the body's major organs, the liver is by far the largest, weighing in at 1.5 kg (3½ lbs) in an adult. This weight is thoroughly deserved, for the liver is the body's chemical miracle worker. Even one of the tasks performed by the liver would pose a severe challenge for an industrial chemist. Yet the liver performs hundreds of these tasks.

The liver is, for instance, a remarkable purification plant, sweeping the blood clean of old red cells and a whole range of poisonous elements such as alcohol. It does not actually make new blood cells itself—that is done in the bone marrow. But it does manufacture a number of vital proteins for the blood plasma. And it is also the source of bile, the fluid so important in the digestion of fat. Bile is actually a by-product of the breakdown of the haemoglobin from old red cells.

Yet first and foremost, perhaps, the liver is the body's chemical dispatch centre, receiving digested food from the gut, repacking it and releasing it on demand. Its role in the dispatch of glucose, is particularly important. The main outcome of carbohydrate digestion, glucose, is the prime energy source for all cells—for brain cells, it is the only source. Without glucose, we would soon die. Guided by two chemical messengers called insulin and glucagon (see page 75), the liver helps to ensure that the level of glucose in the blood washing over every cell never falls too low.

When glucose is swept into the liver from the portal vein, a number of things may happen to it. Some passes right through and into the main blood circulation; some is changed to a substance called glycogen and stored in the liver; some is converted into special fats and dispatched to storage depots around the body; and some is used by the liver itself to fuel all its work.

Like a charged battery, glycogen in the liver is an instant source of energy for the body. When blood glucose levels are high, glucose is changed into glycogen, charging up the battery. When the blood

Fact file . . .

These are just some of the liver's many functions:

Acts as a dispatch centre for the digestive system

Is the body's prime energy store, holding glucose in the form of glycogen

Packs off excess food energy for long term storage in fatty tissues all over the body

Completes breakdown of protein and stores minerals and vitamins

Clears blood of old red cells and other waste matter

Manufactures bile and blood plasma proteins

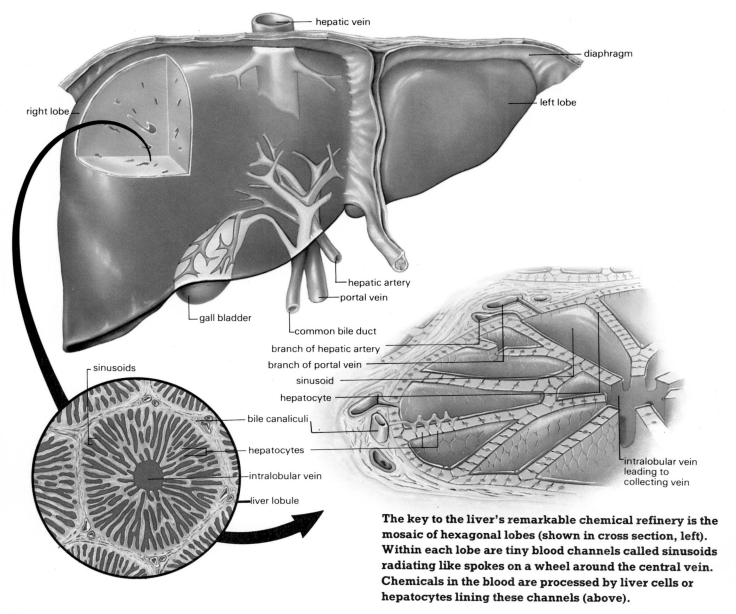

right lobe

hepatic vein

diaphragm

left lobe

hepatic artery

portal vein

gall bladder

common bile duct

branch of hepatic artery

branch of portal vein

sinusoid

hepatocyte

bile canaliculi

hepatocytes

intralobular vein

liver lobule

sinusoids

intralobular vein leading to collecting vein

The key to the liver's remarkable chemical refinery is the mosaic of hexagonal lobes (shown in cross section, left). Within each lobe are tiny blood channels called sinusoids radiating like spokes on a wheel around the central vein. Chemicals in the blood are processed by liver cells or hepatocytes lining these channels (above).

glucose level falls, glycogen is broken down into glucose, giving an instant energy boost for the body. Control of blood glucose levels by the hormones insulin and glucagon is explained in full on page 75.

The stores of fat are energy stores too. But they are long term stores, drawn on only in cases of emergency.

Unlike glucose, the amino acids left after protein digestion cannot be stored by the body. So the liver splits off the useful portion and packs the rest off to the kidneys for disposal, in the form of a fluid called urea. Urea eventually leaves the body in the urine.

HOW THE LIVER WORKS

Unusually, the liver has not one but two blood supplies. Most organs receive blood from an artery alone, but the blood flows into the liver by a vein as well—the portal vein that carries digested food from the gut. Both blood supplies deliver the chemicals to be processed by the liver. There is a third pipe passing through the liver's portal (gateway), but this carries newly-made bile away from the liver to the gut.

Despite the enormous complexity of its tasks, the liver is actually quite simply made. Within the jelly-like

interior of the liver are numerous box-shaped lobes called hepatic lobules—'hepatos' is the Greek for liver, so this just means liver lobes. In each lobe, there are tiny segments, like the segments of oranges. Blood from each of the liver's twin supplies flows in from the outside of each segment, through a channel called a sinusoid, and out through a central vein. As blood flows through the sinusoid, liver cells or hepatocytes lining the walls extract the right elements, process them and return them to the blood. The one exception is bile which goes out the backdoor into the bile duct.

BODY FLUIDS

Besides oxygen and food, the body must receive one more vital input: water. Our need for water is, if anything, even more urgent than our need for food. People have survived more than a month without food; no-one can last more than a few days without water—even less in a hot climate.

A significant loss or gain in water is disastrous. Indeed, the water content of the body must never vary by more than five per cent either way. So the body has a number of mechanisms to ensure that the amount of water remains completely steady.

A crucial factor in the control of water in the body is salt. Water both inside and outside the cells carries a great deal of salt, salt that is vital to many cellular processes. But the balance between the salt carried inside the cell and outside is very delicate. Water inside the cell has a high proportion of potassium chloride. Water outside the cell has more sodium chloride—common salt. An upset in these proportions can spell disaster.

OSMOSIS

The fragile salt balance depends on a special kind of pressure difference between the outside of the cell and the inside. This pressure is called osmotic pressure. Osmotic pressure can occur wherever there is a semi-permeable membrane, such as the skin of the cell. A membrane like this acts as a sieve so fine that water can pass through but salts dissolved in it cannot. When there is more salt in the water on one side of the membrane, water will seep through from the salt-weak side to the salt-strong side until the level of salt is equal. In other words, water moves from an area where there is plenty of water per salt molecule to one where there is less. This movement is called osmosis, and osmotic pressure is the difference in salt levels that provokes it.

The body actually depends on osmosis for transporting fluids across membranes. And the amount of water in each cell is finely controlled by osmotic pressure. The gentle tug-of-war between sodium salts on the outside of the cell and potassium on the inside, pulling water back and forth, ensures that the distribution of water is always just right. But if the fine balance of osmotic pressure is upset, osmosis can be disastrous. If, for instance, the salt level outside the cell rises too high, water is drawn out of the cell. Drained of water, the cell could eventually collapse. On the other hand, if the salt level outside drops too low, water gushes into the cell and the cell blows up like a balloon.

Fortunately, this rarely happens, for the body ensures that the salt concentration is probably maintained within 0.5 per cent. Such precision control is achieved largely by adjusting the amount of water to suit the salt rather than the salt to suit the water.

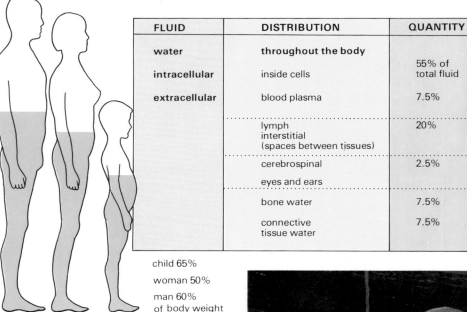

child 65%
woman 50%
man 60%
of body weight

FLUID	DISTRIBUTION	QUANTITY
water	throughout the body	55% of total fluid
intracellular	inside cells	
extracellular	blood plasma	7.5%
	lymph interstitial (spaces between tissues)	20%
	cerebrospinal	2.5%
	eyes and ears	
	bone water	7.5%
	connective tissue water	7.5%

Above: Our bodies contain an enormous amount of water—almost two thirds of our total weight is water. The table shows just where this water goes.

Right: In hot countries, salt lost through sweating is often made up by salty diets to help maintain the fine salt/water balance in the body.

WATER CONTROL

The body gains water in a number of ways—by drinking, by eating and as a by-product of the normal working of the cells (see page 12). It loses water in just as many ways, including sweating, breathing and urinating. Normally, though, the amount of water gained from the cells and lost by breathing and sweating stays relatively stable. So the body controls water content mainly by balancing the water we drink against the water we lose in the urine.

When your body needs more water, your throat feels dry, your stomach may churn a little and you start to feel thirsty. Thirst is one of those sensations, like hunger, that cannot be pinned down to any particular part of the body. Nor can it be described. You just know that you must drink to quench it. It seems to originate in a tiny bundle of nerves in the brain called the hypothalamus which plays a key role in water control.

When you need more water, the hypothalamus not only makes you feel thirsty; it also sends out signals to the pituitary gland (see page 73). The pituitary, in turn, dispatches a chemical messenger called anti-diuretic hormone (ADH for short) to the kidneys. ADH helps the kidneys to hold on to more water and let less escape in the urine. So by getting you to drink more water and holding on to what it has, the body ensures that body water never drops too low. Should the level ever rise too high, the hypothalamus sends signals to reduce your thirst and the release of ADH.

The hypothalamus relies for information on two kinds of detectors: osmoreceptors and volume receptors. These constantly monitor the water in the blood and ring the alarm bells when the salt concentration rises too high or the volume drops too much.

It is the osmoreceptors that monitor salt concentration, detecting changes in osmotic pressure. If osmoreceptors detect soaring salt concentration, signals go out to make good the lack of water. If salt concentration drops, signals go out to increase urination and restore the balance. But controlling the salt/water balance precisely is not quite enough though, for if the amount of salt in the body varies wildly, so will the amount of water. This is where the volume receptors come in.

Volume receptors measure blood volume by detecting how much the walls of the heart and a few other blood vessels are stretched. If the blood volume drops, we immediately feel thirsty, and drink to restore the loss of water—which is why heavy bleeding makes us feel thirsty. In this way, the volume of water and the concentration of salt are precisely controlled.

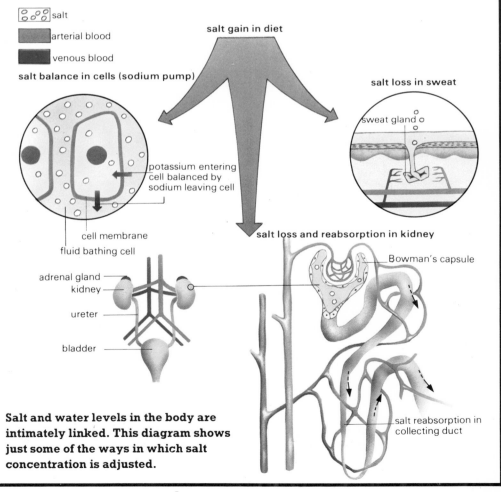

salt

arterial blood

venous blood

salt balance in cells (sodium pump)

salt gain in diet

salt loss in sweat

sweat gland

potassium entering cell balanced by sodium leaving cell

cell membrane

fluid bathing cell

salt loss and reabsorption in kidney

adrenal gland
kidney

ureter

bladder

Bowman's capsule

salt reabsorption in collecting duct

Salt and water levels in the body are intimately linked. This diagram shows just some of the ways in which salt concentration is adjusted.

The kidneys are, as we saw earlier, the key to water control in the body, holding back water or letting it run out as urine. Yet they are much more than just elaborate taps. All this water is mixed in with the blood, and must be drawn off without losing any of the blood's vital ingredients. At the same time, the kidneys must also clear the blood of poisonous waste.

One of the most remarkable things about the kidneys is that they extract water and toxins from blood on the move. Blood slows down as it passes through the kidneys, but does not stop altogether. Blood flows through the kidneys at the rate of 1.3 l (2½ pts) a minute. So in the space of ten minutes or so, all the body's blood has been through the kidneys. And during the course of a day, every drop of blood will have gone through a hundred times, getting cleaner and cleaner as toxins are gradually extracted.

In a way, the kidneys are high-speed filtration plants, for they remove all the unwanted ingredients from the blood by allowing them to escape through a fine mesh. Then they carefully re-absorb the valuable ingredients from the filtrate so that only useless and toxic substances are allowed to escape. The kidneys' precision and care in re-absorption is clear from the fact that out of 170 l (300 pts) of filtrate—and more than 2000 l (3500 pts) of blood—every day, less than 1.2 l (2 pts) are released as urine.

HOW KIDNEYS WORK

The kidneys' accuracy in filtration and re-absorption depends on their million or so individual filtration plants called nephrons. Each nephron consists of an incredibly intricate network of tubes—rightly named convoluted tubules—enclosed in an even more intricate network of blood capillaries. It is here that selective reabsorption into the blood takes place.

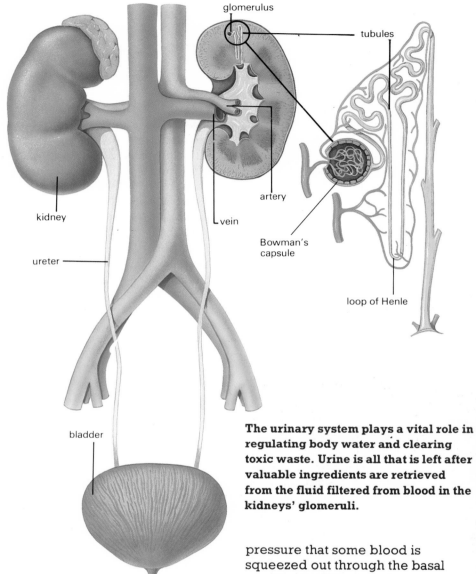

The urinary system plays a vital role in regulating body water and clearing toxic waste. Urine is all that is left after valuable ingredients are retrieved from the fluid filtered from blood in the kidneys' glomeruli.

Blood is fed into each nephron through a little bundle of capillaries called the glomerulus. Like a ball of wool in a cup, the glomerulus is enclosed by the Bowman's capsule and in between the two, there is a thin layer of basement membrane. It is the basement membrane which is the filter.

Blood flows into the glomerulus through one arteriole and out through another, much smaller one. Because the blood flow is suddenly constricted in the glomerulus, it is under considerable pressure—such pressure that some blood is squeezed out through the basal membrane. However, large molecules are too big to squeeze through the minute holes in the membranes and are retained in the blood. So too are the blood cells. Only the very smallest molecules filter through into the Bowman's capsule—water, salts, minerals, glucose, urea (waste from the breakdown of proteins in the liver) and creatinine (waste from muscle metabolism). These molecules dissolved in water form the filtrate.

From the Bowman's capsule, the filtrate trickles into the winding passage of the tubule. Here, energetic cells in the tubule wall retrieve all the amino acids and the glucose from the filtrate and a good 70 per cent of the salt. Meanwhile, the blood flows on from the glomerulus into tiny capillaries that cling to the sides of the tubule. So all the valuable ingredients saved from the filtrate go straight back into the blood. As the concentration of salts in the blood rises again, so too does the osmotic pressure. And as the salt is carried across into the blood, water is drawn after it.

Further on down the tubule, the depleted filtrate runs into a narrow hairpin bend called the loop of Henle. As it squeezes round the bend, the tubule cells retrieve almost all the rest of the salt and return it to the blood. The amount of water re-absorbed in the tubules depends on the water control mechanisms described on page 33.

THE URINE

By the time the filtrate has been through another set of winding tubules and trickled into the collecting duct, there is hardly any left. Of the 125 ml (¼ pt) that enters through the glomeruli each minute, barely 1 ml (1/500 pt) is left to become urine. All the amino acids and all but a faint trace of salt have been re-absorbed into the blood. So too has all the glucose, unless there is an excess in the blood, which can occur in diabetes. All that is left is a little water and the toxic wastes that have been removed from the blood. It is this remnant of filtrate that forms the urine.

Urine is 96% water; the remaining 4% is the toxic wastes that give it its distinctive straw-colour. If

you drink a lot of water, the kidneys release an even higher proportion of water to maintain the body's balance, so the urine is very pale in colour. A dark colour usually indicates an infection.

From the kidneys, urine drains through two narrow pipes called ureters into the bladder. The bladder is essentially an expansible reservoir for urine, holding on to it, usually, until it is convenient to urinate.

At the exit to the bladder are two rings of muscles called sphincters that act like taps. When urine trickling from the ureters fills the bladder warning messages are sent to the brain and the first sphincter opens automatically. The second is under conscious control. When you are ready, you relax this sphincter to let urine flow out.

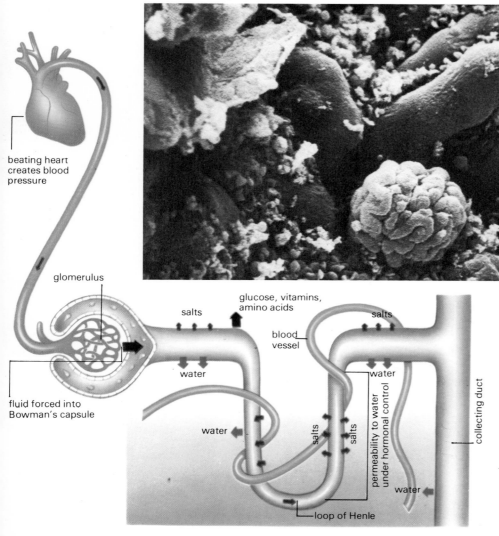

beating heart creates blood pressure

glomerulus

fluid forced into Bowman's capsule

salts

glucose, vitamins, amino acids

blood vessel

salts

water

water

water

salts

salts

permeability to water under hormonal control

collecting duct

water

loop of Henle

Above: A microscope view of a dissected kidney, showing the little knot of blood vessels that make the glomerulus.

Left: The diagram on the left shows how a nephron works. Fluid is filtered from the blood in the glomerulus. As the filtrate passes through the tubules salt and other ingredients useful to the body are retrieved and returned to the blood, followed by a regulated amount of water, leaving just a trickle of urine (water plus waste products) to run into the collecting ducts.

CHAPTER 2

THE BODY IN MOTION

Standing up, walking and running are only a part of the immensely versatile repertoire of movements made by the human body. Its power of movement is based firmly on a strong bony skeleton, to which are attached many muscles that supply the force needed for movement.

Every move the human body makes —from a twitch of an eyebrow to the powerful stride of an olympic hurdler— depends on the same remarkable combination of bone and muscle.

MOVING PARTS

The skeleton is the body's living framework. This intricate scaffolding of more than 200 bones not only supports the tissues and protects the organs; it also provides a vital anchorage point for the muscles.

But the skeleton is more than just a framework. It is a living, active organ. The word skeleton actually comes from the Greek word meaning dried, but the bones are anything but dry. Each bone is full of living cells called osteocytes, entombed in caverns called lacunae, but bathed in blood just like any other body cell. Sometimes osteocytes do die, leaving empty lacunae to fill with salts. Even these are valuable, acting as the body's prime mineral storehouses.

The hollow centres of some bones are even more active, creating new blood cells. There in the soft, spongey red marrow of the breastbone, ribs and hips, millions of red blood cells and white cells are being born every second.

Nevertheless, bone does make a good framework because it is so tough and light; bone accounts for barely 14 per cent of our body weight.

BONE STRUCTURE

Bone depends for its strength on a unique combination of flexibility and stiffness. The flexibility comes from the tough ropelike fibres of collagen. The word collagen comes from the Greek 'kolla' meaning glue and 'gen' meaning forming and it is collagen that holds the

The combination of joints gives the human skeleton a remarkable mobility. Ball and socket joints such as hip and shoulder (a) give free movement in many directions. Hinge joints like knees and elbows (b) can swing in a single plane. The swivel joint between the skull and spine (c) lets you swivel your head. Plane joints such as those in the spine (d) give restricted movement in all directions.

bone together. The rigidity comes from the hard mineral deposits that surround the collagen. Collagen is found throughout the body, but it is the combination of collagen and minerals, especially calcium, that makes bones so tough. Without calcium, bones would be as bendy as rubber; without collagen, they would be brittle as biscuits.

Yet bones undoubtedly owe some of their strength to their marvellous internal structure, seemingly designed to perfection to take stresses and strains in the best possible way. In the long bones of the limbs, for instance, the shaft is not just solid bone. Under a tough coating, there is a compact mass of interweaving rods called osteones running the length of the shaft spreading any stress. And inside this is the marrow,

synovial joint

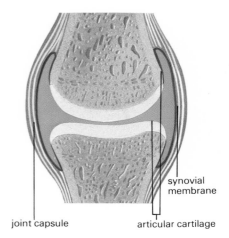

joint capsule

synovial membrane

articular cartilage

A capsule of slippery fluid held in a sleeve of collagen between the bone ends allows the sinovial joints of the limbs to take tremendous weight yet give completely smooth, free movement.

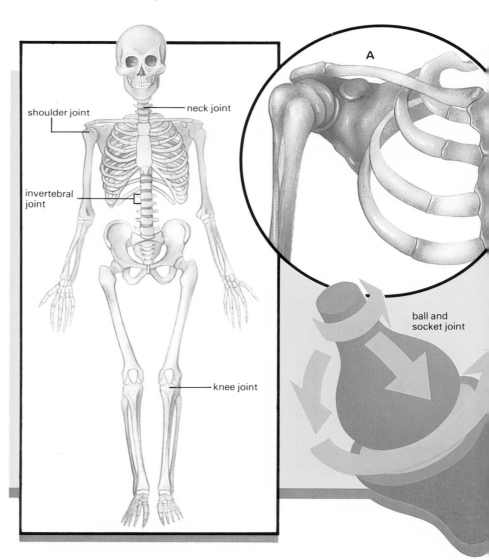

shoulder joint

neck joint

invertebral joint

A

knee joint

ball and socket joint

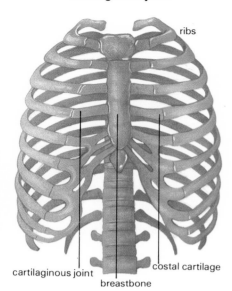

cartilaginous joint

ribs

cartilaginous joint

breastbone

costal cartilage

In cartilaginous joints, a layer of tough cartilage provides plenty of support but restricts movement. This is ideal in the ribs and spine where no single joint needs to move much.

crisscrossed by a delicate tracery of bone filaments called trabeculae. Trabeculae also fill out the foam-like bonehead. They may look fragile, but each trabecula is perfectly angled to resist stresses.

MOBILITY

One of the most remarkable things about the skeleton is that in achieving this strength it does not sacrifice mobility. In fact, the human skeleton is perhaps the most infinitely flexible of all mammals.

To allow this degree of mobility, the skeleton has dozens of joints, each one giving a particular range of movement. The diagram below shows just some of the different types of movement allowed by the joints. There are joints called fibrous joints bound so tightly together with fibres that no movement is possible. Such joints

are found only in the skull. Every other joint in the body moves; some easily in almost any direction, like the shoulders; others just a small way back and forth.

Cartilaginous joints—joints linking the bones with a layer of cartilage (see page 40)—are stiff but provide good support. The joints of the spine are of this type. Yet there are so many that we can actually bend some way—at least until we're old.

Synovial joints allow almost unlimited movement. They are covered in a sleeve of tough collagen fibre. But inside this sleeve is a capsule of sinovial fluid, a lubricant to match the best man-made oils. When a joint such as the knee bends, the bone ends glide over this slippery fluid, but are kept safely apart.

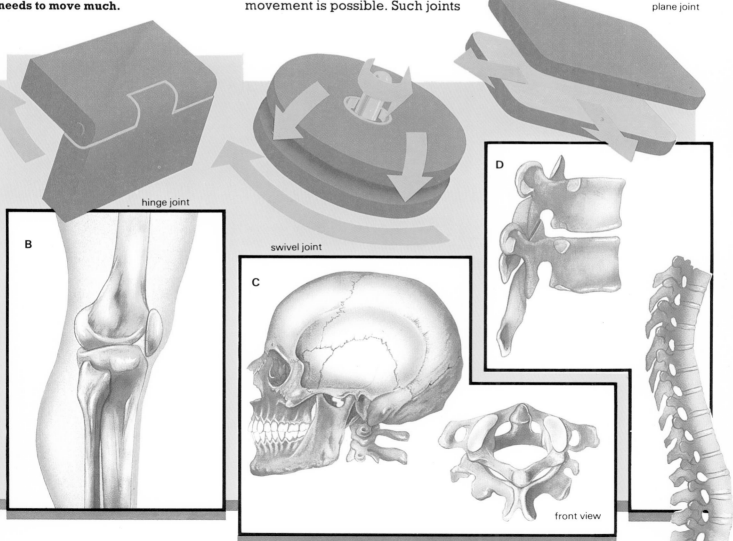

hinge joint

swivel joint

plane joint

B

C

D

front view

JOINTS

Joints are the skeleton's weak points, and the body provides them with as much protection as possible. Some joints are filled with cartilage, as we have seen, and others with synovial fluid. But because of the hardness of bone, cartilage plays a part in nearly every articular (jointed) surface, forming a smooth, flexible protective cover over the rough bone ends.

One reason why cartilage is such ideal joint material is that it is very slippery. With its 'coefficient of

Below: Cartilage owes its pliability to the mixture of collagen and elastin. Tough, fibrous knee cartilage has most collagen. Hyaline cartilage in joints has less but is still tough. Elastic cartilage has much more elastin and is soft and flexible.

Damage to the fibrous cartilage of the knee can be a persistent and painful problem for some footballers.

friction' of 0.013, it is three times more slippery than ice. So like frictionless nylon bearings in machines, cartilage allows joints to glide back and forth with the barest minimum of rubbing.

Cartilage also makes a superb shock absorber. Whenever a joint, such as the hip, knee or ankle, takes any weight, the cartilage is squashed a little and takes some of the strain. As soon as the weight is removed, the cartilage springs smoothly back into shape. In fact, cartilage depends on constant squashing and springing back for its nutrient supply. Unlike most other tissues, the cartilage in the joints does not have its own blood vessels. Instead, it absorbs fluid from the blood vessels of the surrounding tissues. Just like a sponge, it draws in fluid as it springs back into shape. Constant weight on the joints can sometimes be damaging because the cartilage is prevented from bouncing back and drawing in nutrient-rich fluid. For the same reason, long disuse of the joint can be equally damaging.

Healthy articular cartilage owes its resilience to the materials it is

DIFFERENT TYPES OF CARTILAGE

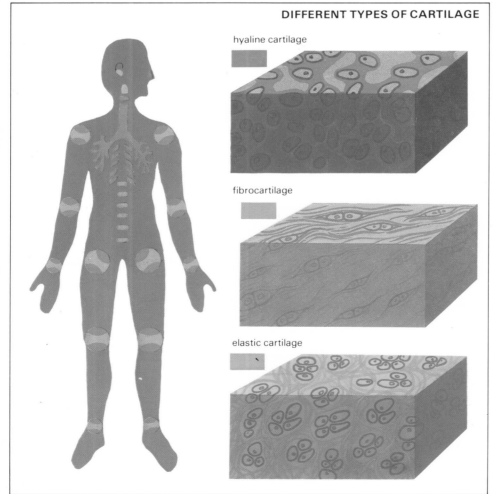

hyaline cartilage

fibrocartilage

elastic cartilage

made of. It is essentially a jelly-like substance given extra firmness by fibres of collagen and elastin. The collagen in cartilage is the same tough ropelike material found in bones. Elastin is, as its name suggests, a much softer, more stretchy material.

Despite the web of fibres and some special cells called chondrocytes, the cartilage in joints looks completely clear. It is this clarity which gives this type of cartilage its name, hyaline cartilage, from the Greek word 'hyalos' meaning glass.

Fact file . . .

Even walking places the thigh bone under a pressure of 3500 kg/cm² (1200 lbs per sq in).

Bones shrink with disuse: in the weightlessness of space, Apollo astronauts lost 4 g (¹/₇ oz) worth of bone a month.

Cartilage is three times more slippery than ice.

KINDS OF CARTILAGE

Cartilage is such a useful material that the body uses it in other places besides the joints. Hyaline cartilage is used in the ribs as well as joints. But there are two other types of cartilage, fibrous and elastic cartilage, used wherever firm support is needed but bone is too hard and stiff.

Fibrous cartilage is found only around the knee. It is firmer than hyaline cartilage, containing more collagen, and is opaque. At the knee, it forms the half-moon shaped pads that footballers sometimes damage. These pads are attached to the thigh bone and shin bone and smooth the action of the knee. They are usually damaged when a footballer is tackled at the moment his weight is fully carried on a bent knee, tearing the cartilage.

Elastic cartilages, as their name suggests, contain more elastin than either hyaline or fibrous cartilage, and are much more flexible. This flexibility makes it the ideal support for the airways. It is also elastic cartilage that makes your nose bendy and your ears flappy.

LIGAMENTS

Adding to the protection to the joints provided by cartilage are tough fibrous cords called ligaments. They are attached to the bone casing either side of the joint and anchor it in place. They are fairly elastic and allow the joint to move freely, but they help prevent it bending too far or twisting sideways. Nearly all the major joints are supported by firm bands of ligaments.

They do sometimes give problems. A sprained ankle, for instance, is usually a tear in the ligaments supporting the ankle. But for the price of a little discomfort, the joint is saved from much more serious damage.

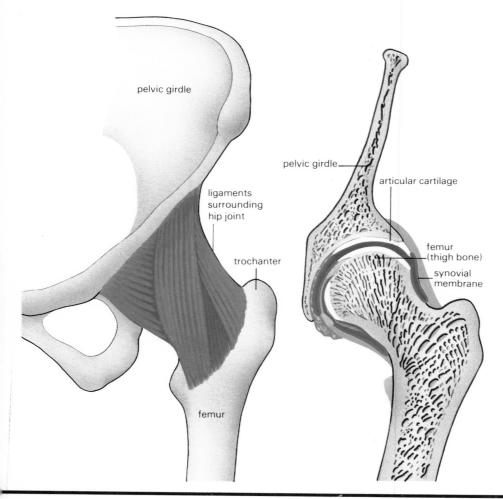

pelvic girdle

ligaments surrounding hip joint

trochanter

femur

pelvic girdle

articular cartilage

femur (thigh bone)

synovial membrane

Running and jumping places the hip joint under enormous stress. The support provided by ligaments (far left) combined with the lubricating cushion of cartilage between the bone ends (left) provide vital protection.

MUSCLE POWER

Every move you make needs muscles. You need muscles to move your leg. You need muscles to twitch an eyebrow. You even need muscles to sit still—for without muscles to hold the body upright, you would slump like a corpse.

There are well over 600 muscles in the body under your control, each one a powerhouse of especially energetic cells. And the sheer range of movements that the muscles enable us to make seems almost infinite.

MUSCLES AND MOVEMENT

Remarkably, muscles achieve this enormous range of movements simply by contracting and relaxing. In other words, each muscle moves the body just by pulling two points together. So every muscle must be anchored at both ends. Many muscles are attached to the bone either side of a joint, either directly or by a set of fibres called tendons. The biceps, for instance, is attached at one end to the radial bone of the lower arm and at the other to the shoulder. When it contracts, the lower arm is pulled towards the shoulder and raised.

Although muscles can shorten themselves, they cannot make themselves longer. Each time a muscle contracts to make a movement, it must be pulled back to its original length by another muscle. So muscles are often arranged in opposing pairs, a flexor muscle to bend or 'flex' a joint and an extensor muscle to straighten it out again. In the upper arm, the biceps is the flexor that bends the arm; the triceps at the back is the extensor that straightens it.

Not all muscle work involves movement. Sometimes a muscle may have to contract just to keep something in the same place. When the muscle moves part of the body, it is called an isotonic (same force) contraction; when the muscle works to simply hold part of the

body in place, it is called an isometric (same length) contraction, because the muscle does not actually get shorter.

You control consciously most of the muscles you need to move or hold still, and so these muscles are called voluntary muscles. But each voluntary muscle needs a nerve signal from the brain to prod it into action—unless the movement is a reflex (see page 62), in which case the nerve signal may come from the spinal cord.

Most movements involve the co-ordinated contraction of many different muscles, so the brain sends a volley of signals down nerves connected to all the right muscles. Each muscle-firing nerve (called a motor nerve) ends next to the muscle in a blob called a motor end plate. The signal is then passed across a tiny gap to the muscle by a chemical messenger that triggers the muscle into action.

HOW MUSCLE WORKS

Muscles owe their power to a unique kind of cell, a cell with not just one nucleus but ten or more. A single cell makes one long fibre

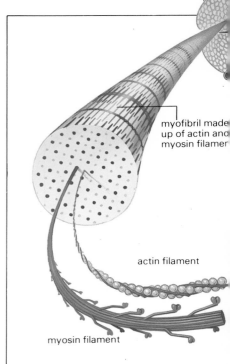

In the muscles you use for movement are thousands of fibres, each made from many thinner fibres called myofibrils. Myofibrils in turn are made from tiny filaments of actin and myosin. These filaments are responsible for a muscle's ability to contract.

myofibril made up of actin and myosin filament

actin filament

myosin filament

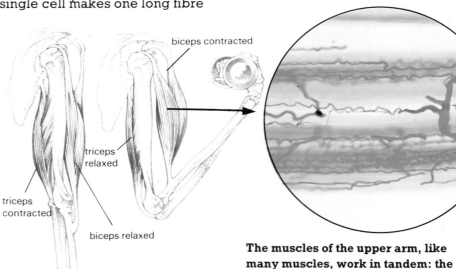

biceps contracted

triceps relaxed

triceps contracted

biceps relaxed

The muscles of the upper arm, like many muscles, work in tandem: the triceps contracts to pull the arm straight (far left): the biceps bends it (left). The photographs (above and right) show this muscle in close up—the stripes made by the filaments are clearly visible (right).

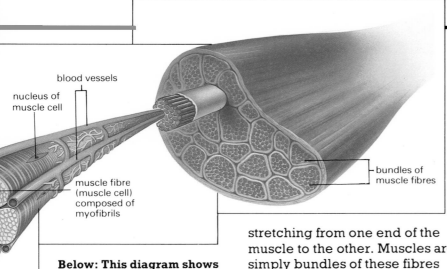

blood vessels

nucleus of
muscle cell

muscle fibre
(muscle cell)
composed of
myofibrils

bundles of
muscle fibres

Below: This diagram shows how the interlocking filaments of actin and myosin (top) draw closer together (bottom) to shorten a muscle.

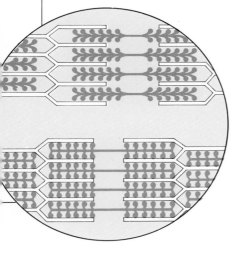

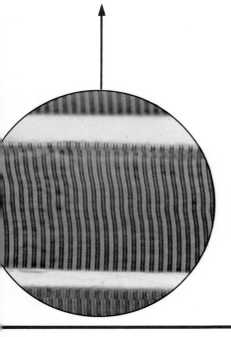

like fingers all the way along the fibril. When a muscle fibre receives a signal to contract, little buds on each myosin filament twist sharply backwards. As they twist, they drag the actin filaments along with them like a log over rollers. This draws the actin filaments sharply right in between the myosin filaments. The effect is that the two kinds of filament are brought suddenly closer together all the way along the muscle fibre. So the fibre shortens dramatically, perhaps by almost half its length.

INVOLUNTARY MUSCLES

Although you consciously control most surface muscles (the voluntary muscles), many muscles on the inside of the body work all by themselves. Some buddhist monks are believed to be able to influence the way these muscles work. But for most of us they are involuntary, contracting and relaxing entirely automatically.

Involuntary muscles fall into two categories: smooth muscle and cardiac muscle. Cardiac muscle is the muscle of the heart that beats by itself (see page 16). Smooth muscle is involved almost anywhere there is movement inside the body. It is smooth muscle that propels food through the gut, for instance, in waves of peristaltic contraction (see page 27). And smooth muscle regulates the flow through the blood vessels. It is called smooth muscle because it is made from flat sheets of muscle cells rather than long fibres like striated muscles.

stretching from one end of the muscle to the other. Muscles are simply bundles of these fibres bound tightly together, like the strands of a telephone cable. Some muscles are made from just a few hundred fibres; other contain more than a quarter of a million.

But just as each muscle is made from hundreds of long thin strands, so is each muscle fibre. The thin strands in muscle fibre are known as myofibrils.

With a powerful microscope, you can see a series of dark bands running round each myofibril. These bands line up so perfectly across the myofibrils that the whole muscle fibre looks stripey. It is these distinctive stripes that give voluntary muscle another name: striated muscle, which means striped muscle—there are other types of muscle, as we shall see later.

With an even more powerful electron microscope, you could see these stripes are really alternating bands of tiny filaments made of actin and myosin. Muscle gains its power to contract from the way the actin and myosin filaments interlock

Fact file . . .

If all the muscles of the body pulled together, they could lift a double-decker bus.

The body has over 600 different voluntary muscles.

Muscle fibres can contract by up to 50 per cent.

PEAK PERFORMANCE

Like a car's engine needs fuel so the muscles need energy. Indeed, when you are working hard they need more energy than the rest of the body put together. Sitting down doing nothing, an average person may get through about 7000 kJ (1700 calories) a day. But as soon as you start even the lightest activity, such as walking or cycling, the body's energy needs rise dramatically.

Muscles get their energy from a number of different sources, but it all ends up in the form of a chemical called adenosine triphosphate (ATP). ATP is the spring in the myosin buds that uncoils to pull the muscle filaments together. But before it can uncoil, it must first be coiled up.

When it uncoils, ATP loses one of its three phosphate atoms to become adenosine diphosphate (ADP). It is loaded again by adding on the phosphate atom. But adding this extra atom requires energy. Much of this energy comes from burning glucose supplied by the blood along with oxygen. In most body cells, this simply pushes on the extra phosphate atom. But in muscles, the energy can also be

Above: During a long race, the muscles of an athlete can work mainly aerobically. But the oxygen supplied by the blood may not be enough for a final dash to the finishing line. So the muscles switch rapidly over to anaerobic activity, drawing on their own reserves of glycogen for a last burst of power.

Right: Jogging is an increasingly popular form of exercise. Providing the run lasts more than a few minutes, it is aerobic. This means that the muscles use oxygen to burn glucose. Regular aerobic exercise improves fitness by building up the body's capacity to supply the muscles with oxygen—lungs grow larger, and the heart beats stronger and more slowly.

Although heart and lung fitness are the most valuable benefits of regular exercise, there can be other positive effects as well. Exercise that thickens the muscle fibres, for instance, makes you stronger. The table shows how different sports have a different combination of benefits. The scales of fitness and energy consumption are graduated from one to five, with five as the most effective or highest.

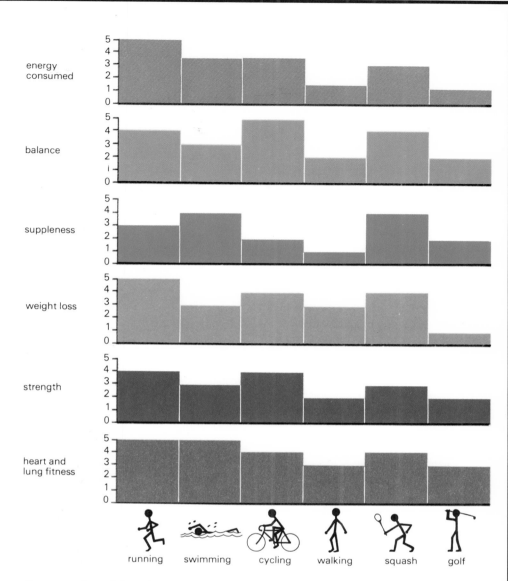

energy consumed · balance · suppleness · weight loss · strength · heart and lung fitness

running   swimming   cycling   walking   squash   golf

stored by forming a chemical called phosphoryl creatine (PCr). This chemical provides an instant source of energy to make ATP. This ready supply is vital, for muscles must be able to work hard instantly.

However, the store of phosphoryl creatine in each muscle is limited. If the muscle is to go on working, the store must be continually topped up by the burning of glucose. With gentle exercise, the bloodstream can deliver fresh supplies of oxygen and glucose to the muscle quite fast enough to keep the store topped up. But as the muscles begin to work harder, the supply of oxygen especially begins to lag. The problem is made more acute by the fact that as the muscle grows tauter, it tends to restrict the blood vessels—so the blood supply is reduced just when the muscles need it most.

ANAEROBIC RESPIRATION

If you go on working the muscle hard, the muscle can burn glucose without oxygen, a process called anaerobic respiration (respiration without air). And if glucose begins to run out too, the muscle may turn for energy to glycogen, its canned form of glucose. It may even start to burn up fat.

The problem with both anaerobic respiration and anaerobic glycolysis (the burning of glycogen) is that they are very inefficient. Each molecule of glucose provides up to 18 times less useful energy than normal aerobic respiration—that is, with oxygen.

A second problem is that instead of leaving carbon dioxide and water like aerobic respiration, anaerobic respiration leaves lactic acid. It is the build-up of lactic acid that makes overworked muscles feel sore.

Once the burst of muscle activity is over, all the lactic acid created by anaerobic respiration must be converted back to glucose in the liver. This re-conversion process needs a great deal of oxygen. So immediately you stop running, for instance, you start panting rapidly as the lungs try to take in more oxygen. During the run, the muscles have, by anaerobic respiration, built up a debt of oxygen which must be repaid as soon as you stop running.

AEROBIC EXERCISE

The way muscles use energy during exercise varies tremendously according to the exercise. But most exercise starts with a brief period of anaerobic respiration. Your muscles need energy instantly. There is not enough time to increase the oxygen supply to meet this sudden increase in demand. So they burn glucose without air. But as long as the activity is not too strenuous, the oxygen intake will soon build up. And, within a few minutes, nearly all the energy can be supplied aerobically. So any exercise that goes on past the initial anaerobic stage is aerobic.

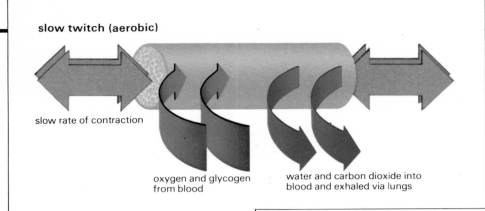

slow twitch (aerobic)

slow rate of contraction

oxygen and glycogen from blood

water and carbon dioxide into blood and exhaled via lungs

The two red fibres can be distinguished by the way they twitch. A twitch is a single contraction of the fibre. One kind of red fibre twitches slowly; the other twitches rapidly.

Slow-twitch red fibres are thin and easily supplied with blood, and they contain a red-coloured substance called myoglobin which

Slow-working, slow-twitch red muscle fibres can go on contracting for a long time without tiring because they work aerobically (above). But they cannot provide instant power. In contrast, fast-twitch white fibres give an instant burst of power by drawing on internal energy sources, mainly glycogen (right). But they are soon exhausted by a build-up of lactic acid (below).

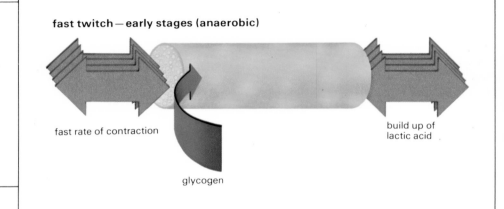

fast twitch — early stages (anaerobic)

fast rate of contraction

glycogen

build up of lactic acid

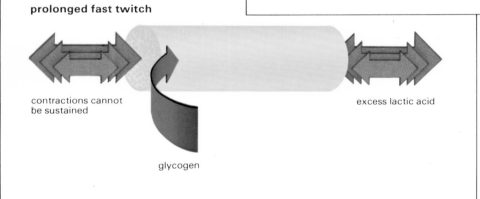

prolonged fast twitch

contractions cannot be sustained

glycogen

excess lactic acid

Below: Regular exercise dramatically improves the body's ability to adapt to exercise. A comparison of the effects of different activities on the heart rate before and after a training period is shown in the graph.

The time you can go on exercising aerobically depends very much on the activity and how fit you are. Even an unfit person can keep up a gentle stroll for a long time. But running will tire even the fittest person.

Some kinds of exercise demand so much energy that aerobic respiration is not enough. To jump in the air or sprint down a racetrack, for instance, the muscles need instant power. Such brief bursts of activity will be almost entirely anaerobic—which is why you can not keep them up for more than a few seconds. Other less strenuous activities can also be anaerobic,

depending on how fit you are. Trained athletes can work much harder before their muscles start to work anaerobically.

RED AND WHITE MUSCLE

Not all muscles get tired at the same rate. Nor are all muscles so good at providing instant power. This is because they are made from different kinds of muscle fibre.

Scientists have now discovered at least three different kinds of muscle fibre and there may be more. At the moment, two types of red-coloured fibre and one white have been identified.

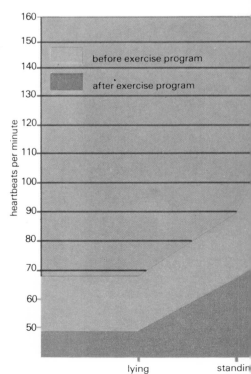

before exercise program

after exercise program

heartbeats per minute

160
150
140
130
120
110
100
90
80
70
60
50

lying   standin

helps carry oxygen. So these fibres are good aerobically. Although they cannot give a burst of rapid action, they can go on slowly twitching for hours without tiring. Muscles that have to keep going for a long time—such as the muscles that hold your back straight—contain a high proportion of slow-twitch red fibres.

White fibres are much thicker and have no myoglobin. When fired, they twitch powerfully and rapidly —but anaerobically. So they are quickly exhausted. Some arm muscles have a high proportion of white fibres, which is why you can

One of the great benefits of regular aerobic exercise is a dramatic improvement in these responses to activity. The body adapts to the regular demand from muscles for more oxygen. A fit person tends to have bigger lungs and a strong heart. Much more blood is pumped round with each stroke, and so the heart beat when resting can be slow and steady. Heart and lung capacity are boosted quickly and easily to cope with the extra demands of strenuous exercise.

A long run has a dramatic effect on an unfit person. He pants rapidly, his heart rate shoots up and he goes red in the face as the blood vessels near the skin widen to help keep him cool (see page 76). He also takes a long time to recover

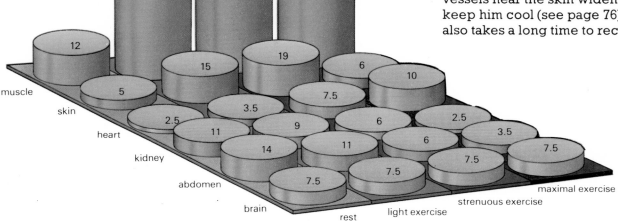

muscle · skin · heart · kidney · abdomen · brain

rest · light exercise · strenuous exercise · maximal exercise

220 · 125 · 45 · 12 · 5 · 2.5 · 11 · 14 · 15 · 3.5 · 9 · 7.5 · 19 · 7.5 · 6 · 11 · 7.5 · 6 · 6 · 10 · 2.5 · 7.5 · 3.5 · 7.5

punch something really hard but only hold a bag of sugar at arm's length for a matter of minutes. Fast-twitch red fibres seem to be a compromise between slow-twitch red fibres and white fibres.

MORE AIR

When your muscles work hard, they need more oxygen to burn glucose. So the body steps up the supply of oxygen to meet the increased demand. It does this in two ways. First of all, your breathing speeds up; you take more and deeper breaths in a minute. Secondly, your heart pumps faster and harder to boost the supply of oxygen-rich blood to the muscles. At the same time, the muscular taps in the arteries open and close to divert this blood to the muscles.

Above: The body adapts to exercise by diverting blood to the muscles. In a gentle stroll, this has only a minimal effect on the rest of the body. But in strenuous and peak activity, the blood supply to the muscles rises sharply while the supply to internal organs such as the kidney is cut back. Only the brain's supply remains steady.

afterwards—primarily because his heart and lung capacity was not enough to keep his muscles supplied with oxygen, and they have built up a huge oxygen debt. In contrast, an athlete's heart and lung capacity have been built up by regular exercise. Hard work will therefore have much less effect on his breathing and heart rate, and he will recover much more quickly afterwards.

climbing stairs · sitting

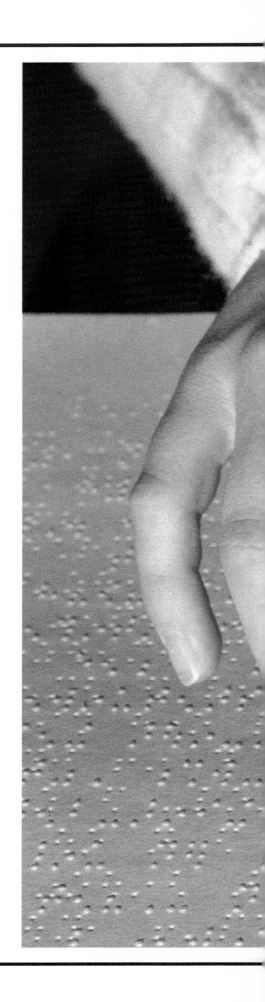

CHAPTER 3

SENSING THE WORLD

Our senses tell us about the world around us. Even when asleep, we are alive to many sensations, some of which come from inside our bodies, others from outside. Nerve messages travel from sense organs to the brain. The brain then gives any orders necessary, in the form of further nerve messages, to target organs such as muscles and glands.

The world at our fingertips—our senses provide us with a constant stream of information about the world. The acute sensitivity of 'touch' allows blind people to read braille letters almost as clearly as sighted people read print.

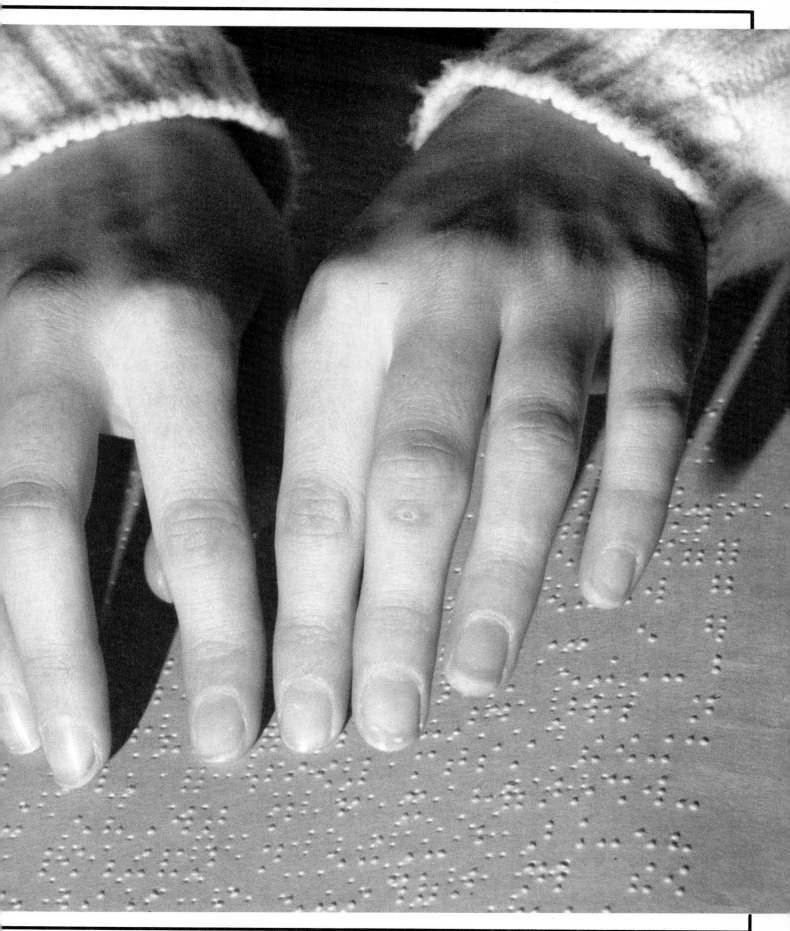

SIGHT

Our eyes are among our most wonderful possessions, combining optical quality and versatility in a way even the best camera cannot equal. The image formed on the back of the eye, the retina, is only a few millimetres across. Yet it seems so big and clear that it never occurs to us that it is just an image.

A high quality glass lens may be able to compete with the eye for sharpness. But no glass lens can combine this kind of sharpness with the enormous focusing range of the eye. A normal eye can focus just as easily on a speck of dust a few centimetres away, as on a distant star, many light years away.

What is more, the eye can see in light varying in brightness from starlight to bright sunlight—a difference in brightness of more than one hundred thousand million times. The eye achieves this remarkable range by adjusting its sensitivity to suit the light—if you walk into a dark room, you will notice how your eyes gradually become accustomed to the light.

LENS AND RETINA

The eye can be divided into two main parts: a lens at the front to form the image; and the retina at the back to record the image.

The lens forms the image by focusing the light rays from each

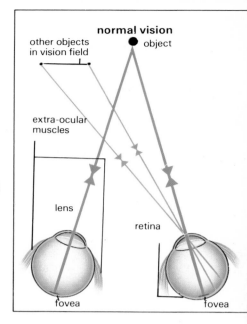

Above: Having two eyes enables us to see in three dimensions (3D) and tell how far away an object is by the tug on the ocular muscles as the eyes turn in to focus on it.

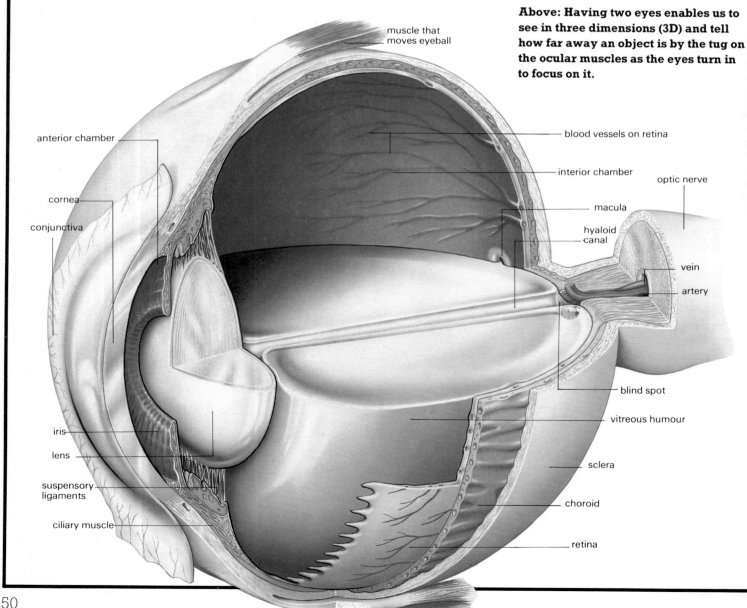

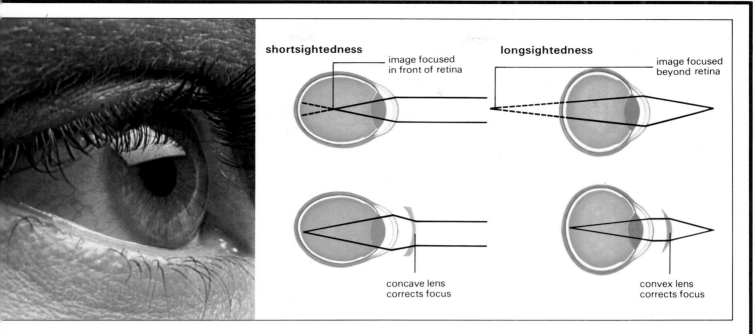

shortsightedness — image focused in front of retina

longsightedness — image focused beyond retina

concave lens corrects focus

convex lens corrects focus

The pupil narrows in bright light to give us a sharper view (above). Shortsightedness occurs when the eyeball is too long (above right). Light rays from a distant object are focused in front of the retina and the image is blurred. This fault can be corrected by wearing concave lenses.

part of the scene on to the retina. Surprisingly, perhaps, the lens that forms the eye's image is not the crystal disc that looks like a camera lens. Instead, it is the clear front cover called the cornea. The crystalline lens simply helps us to focus at different distances. When we wish to focus on something nearby, the ring of ciliary muscle around the crystalline lens tightens to make the lens thicker. When we wish to focus further away, the muscle relaxes and radial muscles stretch and thin the lens out.

Focusing is improved by the pupil, the round window in the centre of the eye. The size of the pupil is varied by the coloured fibres of the iris. When the light is poor, the iris opens the pupil wide to let as much light as possible into the eye. But when the light is bright, the pupil narrows to give the sharpest possible image.

The image is focused on the retina at the back of the eye. The retina has over 130 million light-sensitive receptors that record the pattern of light formed by the image and send signals via optic nerves to the brain. Most of these receptors are clustered in the centre of the retina, in a small dish called the fovea. So although we can see over an angle of more than 140°, we see sharply over only a very narrow angle in the centre of vision.

RODS AND CONES

There are actually two types of receptor in the eye: rods and cones. Rods are very sensitive and work even in the dimmest light, but cannot tell the difference between colours. Cones are responsible for colour vision, but they cease to react in dim light. Colours disappear at night because the cones stop working and we see

Longsightedness (above) is the inability to focus near objects on the retina and can be caused by the eyeball being too short. Light rays are not focused by the time they hit the retina. This complaint can be corrected by wearing convex lenses.

only with rods.

There are, in fact, three different kinds of cone, each reacting to a different band of colour—roughly blue, green and red, though there is considerable overlap. Colour is not real but created in the brain; 'colours' are just different wavelengths of light. The brain sees colour by the relative stimulation of each type of cone. For instance, if the eye receives more red light, the brain sees red—just as if we add red to a mixture of paint it becomes redder.

Fact file . . .

The eye has 125 million rods and 7 million cones.

The eye can vary the sensitivity of the rods by a factor of ten million.

We blink for 0.3 seconds every two to ten seconds.

HEARING

Sounds are nothing more than vibrations in the air—waves of varying pressure rippling out from the sound source. Yet with our ears we are able to detect these vibrations and transform them into all the rich variety of sounds that we hear, from the roar of heavy traffic to the whisper of waves on the seashore.

For most animals, hearing is simply a valuable early warning system. But some scientists believe that human hearing evolved further to allow us to speak to each other. Our ears are indeed especially well-adapted to hearing speech. People with normal hearing can not only distinguish words without even thinking, but can detect subtle variations in tone and accent—and recognize people by their voices.

Hearing has become so important to us that we continually stimulate this sense for pleasure, with music.

THE EAR

To hear all these sounds, the ear channels vibrations in the air via three compartments towards sensitive pressure detectors. The three compartments are: the outer ear, the middle ear and the inner ear.

The outer ear is the collection point for the ear. Sound is gathered by the visible flap we call the ear and funnelled in towards the middle ear. To keep out dirt and insects, the passageway leading inwards is lined with hairs and covered in a yellow wax secreted from glands in the walls.

About two millimetres down the entrance tube, sound suddenly hits a membrane stretched right across the tube. This membrane is the tympanic membrane or eardrum. The eardrum touches the ear's amplifier, three linked bones called the ossicle. When sound strikes the eardrum it vibrates, and as it vibrates it rattles the ossicle. High-pitched sounds vibrate the eardrum (and so the ossicle) very rapidly; low sounds vibrate the drum slowly. In most sounds, though, there is a complex mix of fast and slow vibrations.

The three bones in the ossicle are all known by Latin names that have simple and descriptive English meanings: the malleus (hammer), the incus (anvil) and the stapes (stirrup). When the eardrum vibrates, it rattles the hammer against the anvil and the anvil shakes the stirrup (so called because of its shape).

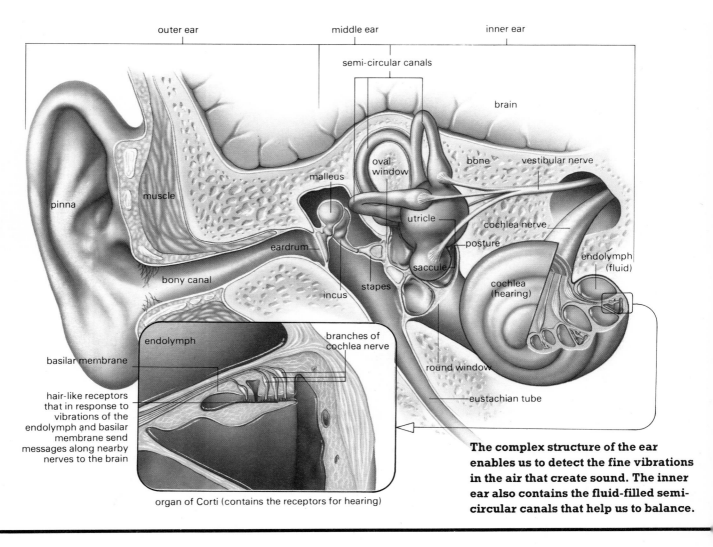

outer ear   middle ear   inner ear

semi-circular canals

brain

oval window

malleus

bone   vestibular nerve

pinna

muscle

utricle

cochlea nerve

eardrum

posture

saccule

endolymph (fluid)

bony canal

stapes

incus

cochlea (hearing)

endolymph

branches of cochlea nerve

basilar membrane

round window

hair-like receptors that in response to vibrations of the endolymph and basilar membrane send messages along nearby nerves to the brain

eustachian tube

organ of Corti (contains the receptors for hearing)

The complex structure of the ear enables us to detect the fine vibrations in the air that create sound. The inner ear also contains the fluid-filled semi-circular canals that help us to balance.

Having two ears enables us to pinpoint a sound, though not always accurately. You can tell which tree the bird is in, for instance. Because one ear is not in direct line with the sound, the bird's whistling is quiet in this ear. The brain analyzes the difference in intensity between the ears and tracks the sound.

Running round and round through the cochlea are three tubes. In the middle tube are long and intricate rows of fine hairs covered by a narrow membrane flap. These rows of minute hairs are called the organ of Corti and this is the real organ of hearing.

When the stirrup knocks on the oval window, it sends pressure waves shooting up around the cochlea. As they run through the cochlea, the pressure waves move the membranes back and forth. And as the membranes move, they tug the hairs of the organ of Corti to and fro, playing upon them like hands gliding swiftly over harp strings. Although the exact mechanism is not completely understood, it seems that the hair cells send nerve signals to the brain as they are tickled. The sound the brain hears depends on which hairs send signals.

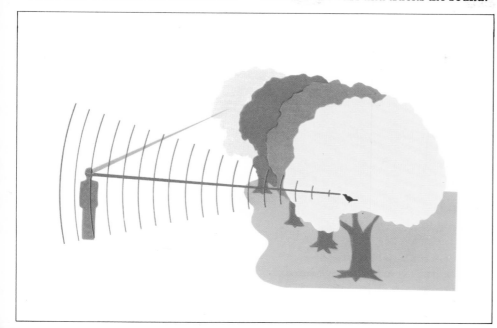

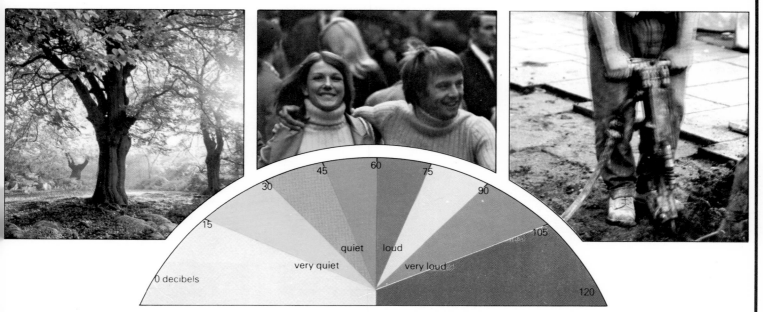

Because of the way they are linked, the bones amplify the sound. The hammer is the biggest of the three bones and moves a long way with each vibration. The stirrup is the smallest and vibrates only a little way, but each vibration is that much stronger. This extra force is vital, for unamplified, the sound waves would not be strong enough to vibrate the fluid in the inner ear.

Amplification is completed as the stirrup rattles on the membrane that covers the entrance to the inner ear, called the oval window. This tough membrane is about 30 times smaller than the eardrum. So the vibration is compressed and intensified.

Beyond the oval window lies the inner ear and a fluid-filled coil of passageways called the cochlea. The cochlea gets its name from the Latin word for snail shell and indeed this is just what it looks like.

The range of sounds we can hear is remarkably wide. Sound intensity is usually measured in decibels on a geometric scale—that is, three decibels are twice as loud as two, and four twice as loud as three. A child with normal hearing can hear sounds from 10 db—quieter than leaves rustling in the trees—to over 140 db, the kind of sound made by a jet engine at close range. But sounds over 100 db can be painful and harmful.

OTHER SENSES

Sometimes called the exteroceptors because they tell us about the world just outside our bodies—our nearby exterior—touch, smell and taste provide a rich and detailed range of information.

TOUCH

Touch is the most widely-spread of all our senses, with receptors all over our bodies, from head to toe. Although some places have many more receptors than others—hands and face, for instance—there is not a square centimetre of skin without some receptors.

The receptors in the skin respond to several different kinds of sensation: a light touch, continuous pressure, heat and cold, and pain. But it is difficult to tell which receptors respond to each kind of sensation. All four kinds of sensation are felt in areas of skin where the only receptors are exposed free nerve ends. Yet in other areas, nerve endings have very definite shapes.

Near the surface of the skin, particularly on the palm side of the fingers, there are little capsules called Meissner's corpuscles which are probably touch sensors. It may

be the fine touch sensitivity of the Meissner's corpuscles that enables us to distinguish delicate textures by feel alone. There are also the hemispherical Merkel's discs which may respond to continuous pressure. Deeper in the skin are the Krause bulbs believed to register cold, the Ruffini endings for temperature change and the very deep pancake-like Pacinian corpuscles which react to vibration and continuous pressure.

When a receptor is stimulated, it fires off nerve signals to the brain. The rate of firing tells the brain how heavy the touch is or how cold it is. But the receptor does not go on firing off signals indefinitely, even if the stimulus continues. Instead, the firing rate steadily falls off as the receptor adapts. Once it has alerted the brain, there is no need to send more than the occasional reminder. This is why we soon cease to feel our clothes after we put them on in the morning, or feel gloves even though the hands are very sensitive.

SMELL

Smell is the most underrated and least understood of all our senses. It is the one sense that man has been completely unable to mimic with machines. Human smell receptors can distinguish between over three thousand different chemicals. They can also detect the faintest traces of chemicals in air.

Our sense of smell seems to rely entirely on a small patch of olfactory receptors inside the top of the nose. This patch is barely 6 cm^2 (1 sq in) and contains five million receptors. These receptors feed into just 15,000 nerve fibres. The secret of the brain's ability to identify smells may lie in the brain, for these nerve fibres lead into a very complex series of connections.

No-one knows quite how smell works. For a smell to reach the nose, it must vaporize so that it can be wafted up the nostrils. It must also dissolve in water so that it can get through the mucus covering the receptors. Yet water vapour itself

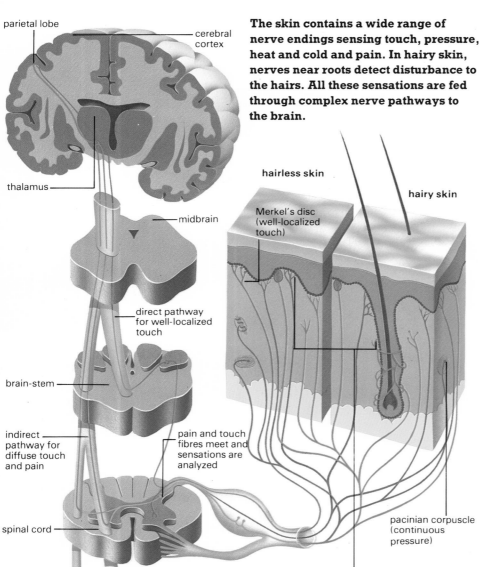

The skin contains a wide range of nerve endings sensing touch, pressure, heat and cold and pain. In hairy skin, nerves near roots detect disturbance to the hairs. All these sensations are fed through complex nerve pathways to the brain.

parietal lobe

cerebral cortex

thalamus

midbrain

direct pathway for well-localized touch

brain-stem

indirect pathway for diffuse touch and pain

pain and touch fibres meet and sensations are analyzed

spinal cord

hairless skin

Merkel's disc (well-localized touch)

hairy skin

pacinian corpuscle (continuous pressure)

free nerve endings (light touch and pain)

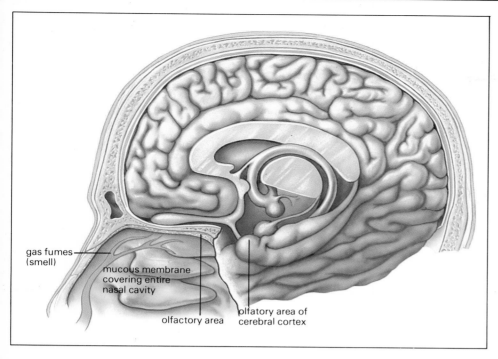

gas fumes (smell)

mucous membrane covering entire nasal cavity

olfactory area

olfatory area of cerebral cortex

the tongue. These respond to four different qualities in the food we eat: sweet, salty, bitter, sour. Sweet detectors are most common near the tip of the tongue; salty, just behind on the sides of the tongue; sour, further back still; and bitter, near the root.

Each of the 10,000 or so taste buds are found inside the pores of some of the tongue's hillock-like papillae. Food dissolved in saliva reaches the taste buds through pores in the papillae. There are 10–20 receptors responding to a mixture of the four tastes in each taste bud. Each activates a nerve leading to the brain. In the brain, the taste signals are mixed with sensations from other kinds of receptor to reveal the full flavour of the food.

Above: Smell is detected by the olfactory receptors at the top of the nose and signals are fed to the olfactory lobe of the brain for analysis.

has no smell. Some scientists have suggested that we can only smell substances made of certain shaped molecules. Most of the chemicals we can smell, for instance, are known to contain at least three atoms of carbon.

Like touch, our sense of smell reacts more to change than to steady stimuli. Quicker even than touch, the nasal receptors adapt to a new odour. To take more than a whiff of the sweet scent of roses, we have to breathe deeply and concentrate hard. Unfortunately, there are some odours our noses are slower to adapt to.

Man may have less need of a sense of smell than other animals, and we depend more on other senses for information about the world. But it still has survival value—in detecting poisonous gases and bad food, for instance. And it has been suggested that smell may play a part in our attraction to the opposite sex. It may be that chemical 'pheromones' in the sweat may help to arouse a potential partner.

The papillae of the tongue (above) contain taste buds that detect sweet, salty, bitter and sour tastes. In some areas, receptors for particular tastes predominate (right).

TASTE

Like smell, taste relies on chemo-receptors. But it is a very indistinct kind of sense. The fine discrimination of the wine taster or the gourmet seem to depend on a mixture of sensations—taste, heat, cold, texture and smell especially.

The only taste receptors the body does have are in the taste buds in

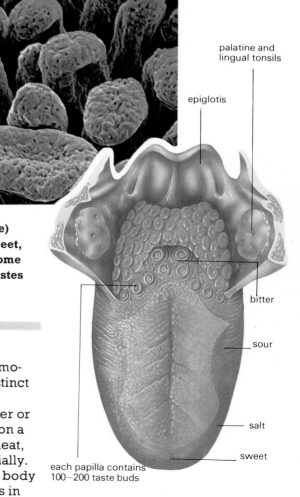

palatine and lingual tonsils

epiglotis

bitter

sour

salt

sweet

each papilla contains 100–200 taste buds

CHAPTER 4

BODY CONTROL

Co-ordinating all the systems of the body—and enabling us to direct our actions—are two remarkable complementary control mechanisms: the nervous system and chemical messengers called hormones. The nerves are the body's hot-lines, carrying instant messages directly to the organs and muscles. Hormones are more like letters, slower and less direct, but longer-lasting.

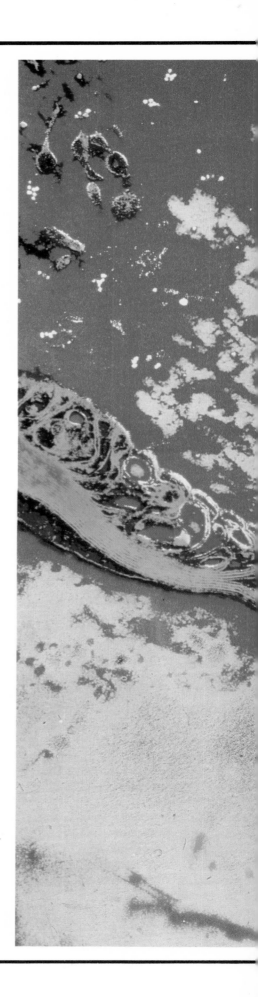

Body control depends on bundles of special cells called 'neurons', shown greatly magnified in the electron microscope picture here.

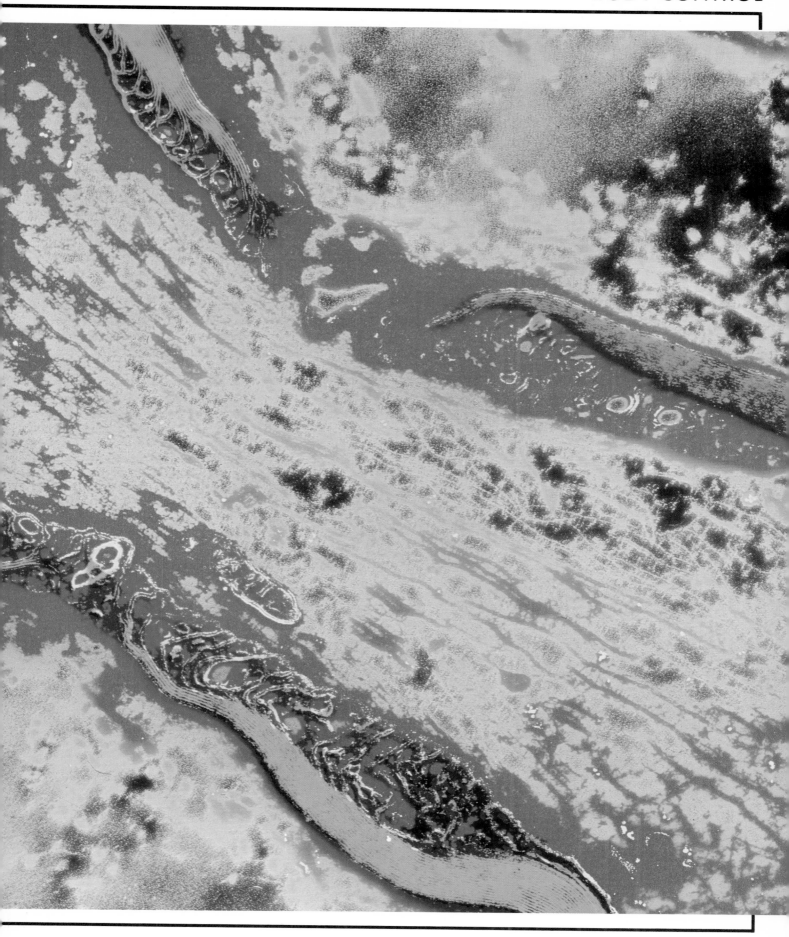

NERVES

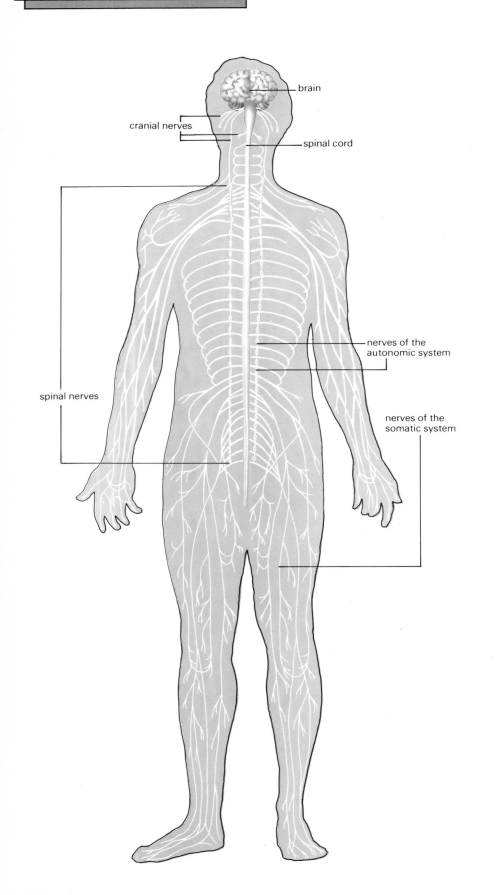

- brain
- cranial nerves
- spinal cord
- nerves of the autonomic system
- nerves of the somatic system
- spinal nerves

Like a busy telephone network, the nervous system is continually alive with activity, buzzing little messages rapidly to and fro all over the body. Every second, hundreds of nerve impulses arrive in the brain with information from the body's sense receptors; equally many leave the brain with instructions for various muscles and organs.

The nervous system centres on the brain and the bundles of nerves running down the spine known as the spinal cord. Together the brain and the spinal cord form the body's central nervous system or CNS. The CNS is the junction box of the nervous system, and every nerve message starts or finishes here. But spreading out from the CNS are hundreds upon hundreds of tiny thread-like nerves that stretch into all corners of the body. These form the peripheral nervous system.

Peripheral nerves carry messages both to and from the CNS, but each nerve can carry messages only one

Left: Nerves radiate all over the body from the spine and the brain, carrying continual rapid pulses to monitor and control our every action.

Below: These neurons in the human brain have been magnified about 200 times actual size.

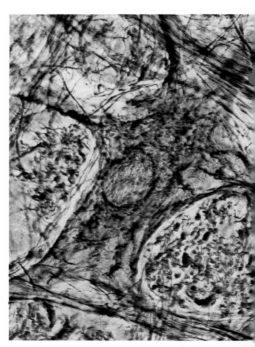

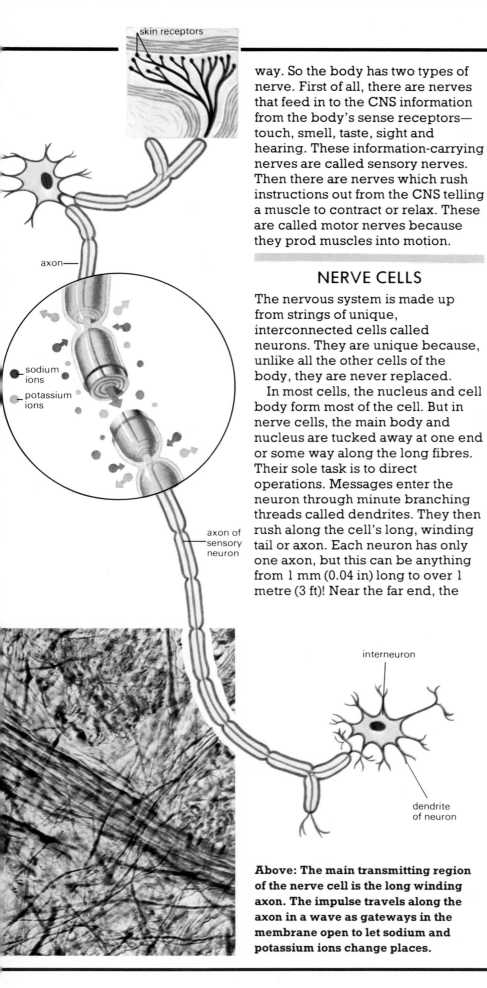

way. So the body has two types of nerve. First of all, there are nerves that feed in to the CNS information from the body's sense receptors—touch, smell, taste, sight and hearing. These information-carrying nerves are called sensory nerves. Then there are nerves which rush instructions out from the CNS telling a muscle to contract or relax. These are called motor nerves because they prod muscles into motion.

NERVE CELLS

The nervous system is made up from strings of unique, interconnected cells called neurons. They are unique because, unlike all the other cells of the body, they are never replaced.

In most cells, the nucleus and cell body form most of the cell. But in nerve cells, the main body and nucleus are tucked away at one end or some way along the long fibres. Their sole task is to direct operations. Messages enter the neuron through minute branching threads called dendrites. They then rush along the cell's long, winding tail or axon. Each neuron has only one axon, but this can be anything from 1 mm (0.04 in) long to over 1 metre (3 ft)! Near the far end, the

Labels on diagram:
skin receptors
axon
sodium ions
potassium ions
axon of sensory neuron
interneuron
dendrite of neuron

Above: The main transmitting region of the nerve cell is the long winding axon. The impulse travels along the axon in a wave as gateways in the membrane open to let sodium and potassium ions change places.

axon splits into hundreds of feathery fibres that pass on the message to the dendrites of other nerve cells.

Just as the cable of a television aerial is surrounded by thick insulation to keep the signal strong, so some nerves are insulated. Nerves that have to carry particularly urgent messages are wrapped in a special myelin sheath. This sheath is actually a series of long, flat cells called Schwann cells wrapped like Swiss rolls around the axon. They insulate nerves so well that impulses travel almost 200 times faster in myelinated nerves than they do in unmyelinated ones.

THE NERVE PULSE

In a way, a nerve is rather like an electric wire. Indeed, it was once thought that the nerve impulse was electrical. But this is only partially true, for the way nerves transmit messages is a remarkable mixture of electricity and chemistry.

The key to the nerve impulse is the electrical difference between the outside and the inside of the neuron. On the outside of the neuron is an excess of electrically-charged sodium ions (particles); on the inside, there is an excess of potassium ions. But the cell membrane normally prevents sodium drifting into the cell and potassium drifting out to equalize the charge—that is, until a nerve impulse arrives. Then minute gateways in the membrane open to allow the sodium ions to move in and the potassium ions out. The entry of sodium into the cell has the effect of opening the gateways in the membrane a little further along the nerve. This, in turn, lets in more sodium which opens gateways even further along the nerve, letting in more sodium. And so the impulse is passed all the way along the nerve. After this impulse has passed, the sodium is soon pumped back out of the nerve—in perhaps a hundredth of a second—and the nerve is ready to carry another message.

BRIDGING THE GAP

Nerve impulses pass from neuron to neuron all around the body, creating an intricate web of signals. Yet no two neurons actually touch. Wherever one neuron connects with another, there is a small gap between them called a synapse. For a nerve impulse to be transmitted to the next nerve, it must somehow leap across this gap.

Our ideas on the way synapses work are changing all the time. At the moment, though, it seems that the impulse can leap the gap either electrically or chemically. When the signal is transmitted electrically, it is rather like the electrical spark leaping the gap in a car's spark plugs. In chemical transmission, special chemicals called neurotransmitters pass the message across. Chemical transmission is the most common means, though recent research has shown that electrical transmission is far more important than was once believed.

CHEMICAL PULSES

Chemical transmission seems to work in the following way. Single droplets of neurotransmitters are stored in minute sacs called vesicles in every nerve ending. When a nerve impulse arrives, the vesicles drift towards the cell membrane and fuse with it. As they fuse, the sacs open and spill their contents into the gap between the two cells, called the synaptic cleft. Once in the cleft, they drift rapidly across to the nerve cell on the far side, called the post-synaptic cell.

On the surface of the post-synaptic cell are special receptor sites. The neurotransmitter slots into these sites like a key into a lock. As the transmitter binds with the receptor site, it excites the cell by opening the gateways in the membrane and letting sodium ions rush in. The change created in the electrical field within the cell sends a nerve impulse shooting through the cell in the way described on page 59. Once the transmitter substance has done its work, it must be removed from the receptor site or it will block the next signal. So it is either destroyed by an enzyme or pumped back to a vesicle.

If every nerve signal was passed on by the synapse, we would be overwhelmed by nerve signals, and the muscles would never stop twitching. So in many synapses, the receiving cell reacts to the transmitter not by passing on the impulse but by blocking it. And some neurons actually release transmitter substances that positively inhibit transmission. Throughout the body, there is a delicate balance between excitement and inhibition at the synapses.

Right: Many nerve impulses are carried across the gap between neurons by special transmitter substances (shown as pyramids).

Below: Treated with formaldehyde, a tangle of nerve endings glows green and reveals the presence of the body's chemical messenger noradrenaline.

One of the reasons why synaptic transmission is so hard to understand is that there are not just two chemicals to transmit messages across the synapses: one for excitement and one for inhibition. There is a whole range. Over 40 different transmitter substances are already known and many more may yet be discovered.

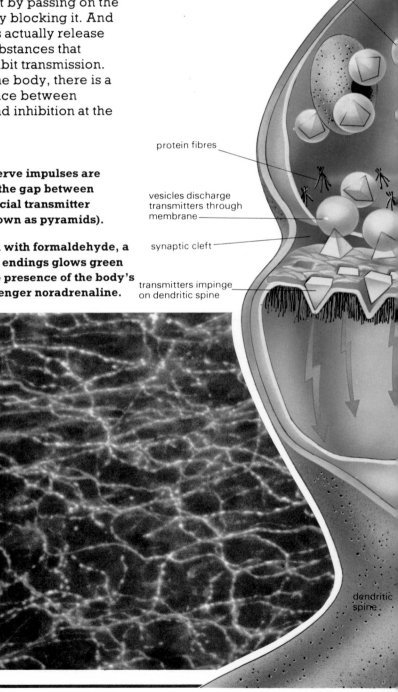

synaptic vesicle

protein fibres

vesicles discharge transmitters through membrane

synaptic cleft

transmitters impinge on dendritic spine

dendritic spine

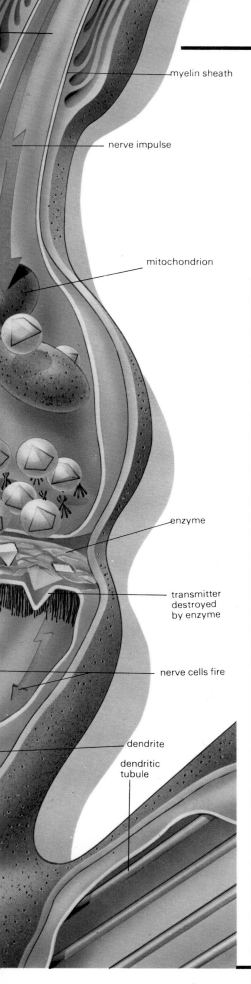

myelin sheath

nerve impulse

mitochondrion

enzyme

transmitter
destroyed
by enzyme

nerve cells fire

dendrite

dendritic
tubule

HOW WE FEEL PAIN

Pain is the body's red alert, warning of damage or impending damage. Some receptors in the skin are specialized for sensing pain, but other receptors also play a part. From the receptors, pain travels through one of two special pathways to the brain (see picture below): a rapid path that probably warns us to avoid further damage; and a slow path that probably acts as a reminder that the damage is still there. En route, however, the pain signal may be considerably modified by the nerve synapses. pain is transmitted across synapses by Substance P, but it is blocked by endorphins and encephalins. The pain-killer morphine may work by mimicking endorphin.

Below: The diagram shows the pathways of pain.

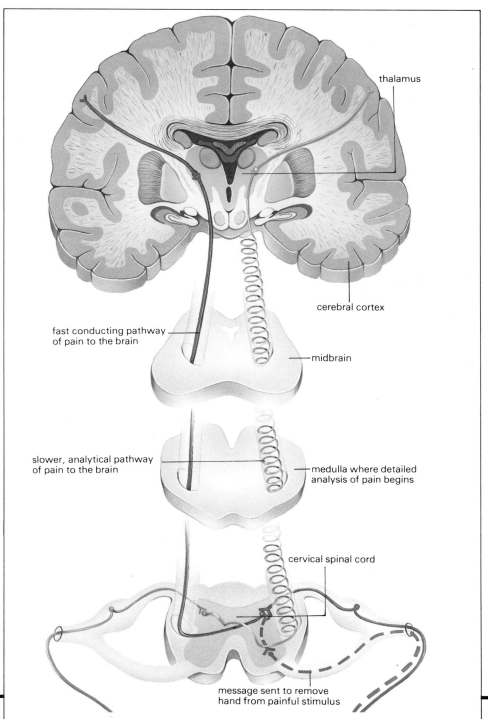

thalamus

cerebral cortex

fast conducting pathway of pain to the brain

midbrain

slower, analytical pathway of pain to the brain

medulla where detailed analysis of pain begins

cervical spinal cord

message sent to remove hand from painful stimulus

THE CNS

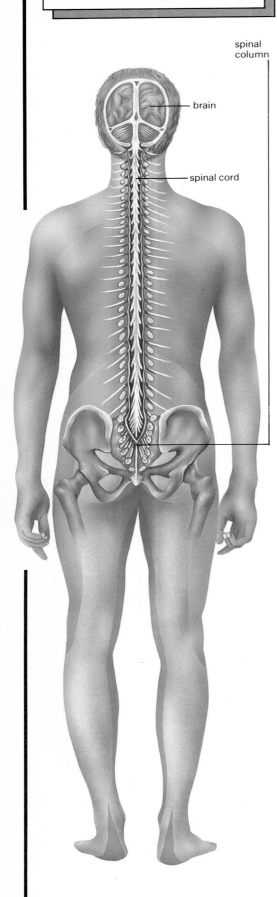

spinal column

brain

spinal cord

The CNS is the core of the nervous system. Together, the nerve cells of the brain and spinal cord process all the information that pours in from the sense receptors and issue the detailed commands needed to prod muscles into action.

Such a precious network clearly needs looking after. So both brain and spinal cord are encased in a tough armour of bone—the brain in the skull and the spinal cord in the spine—and cushioned against shocks by a film of cerebro-spinal fluid and layers of supporting tissue called meninges.

While the brain is the control centre, the spinal cord is the focus of the nervous system. Just twelve cranial nerves, mostly in the head, are linked directly to the brain. All other peripheral nerves are channelled through the spine. Nerves connect with the spine in pairs either side; there are 31 altogether,

one pair for each bone in the back. These 31 nerves can, in fact, be divided into five groups according to the area of the body they serve (see diagram left). Generally, motor nerves and sensory nerves travel through the body together until just before they contact with the spine. There, they split into two, the sensory nerves entering the spinal cord at the back (called the dorsal root) and the motor nerves at the front (the ventral root).

The split in the nerves before they enter the spine provides the key to the body's special emergency response mechanism. If you touch a hot plate, for instance, any delay in removing your hand could cause injury. The time taken for a nerve signal to travel all the way to the brain and receive a response could be disastrous. So the body has developed a system of automatic, lightning fast reactions called reflexes. These happen so quickly that we are only aware of them after the event. They work by short-circuiting the signal sent by the sensory nerve where it enters the spine. An interneuron connects it directly to the right motor nerves, forming a reflex arc.

Nerves leaving different parts of the spine serve different areas of the body (left). With certain sensations, some of these nerves are short-circuited within the spine, giving an instant 'reflex' reaction, such as the knee-jerk (below), to move the body rapidly out of harm.

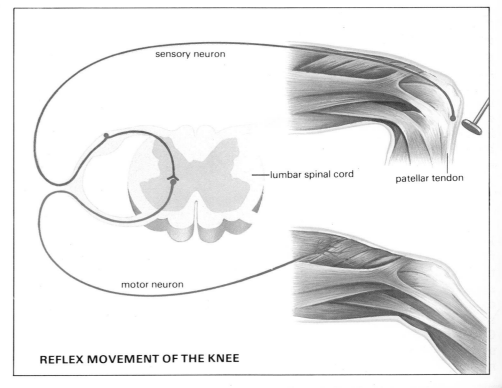

sensory neuron

lumbar spinal cord

patellar tendon

motor neuron

REFLEX MOVEMENT OF THE KNEE

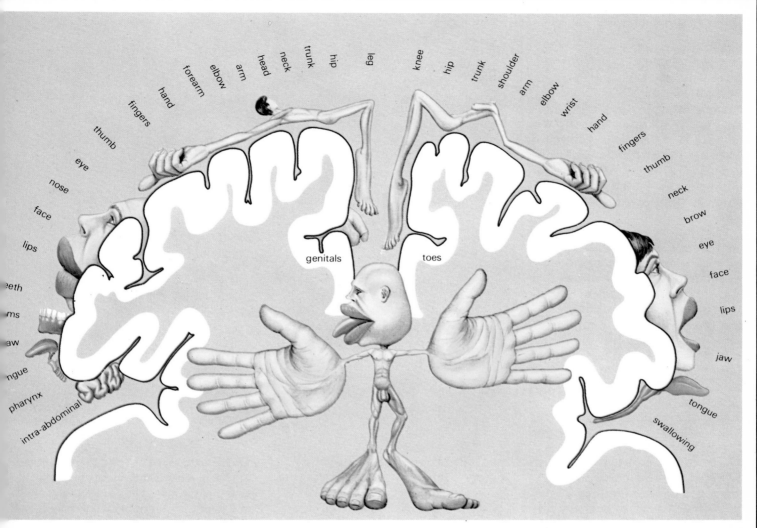

fingers • thumb • eye • nose • face • lips • eeth • ms • aw • ngue • pharynx • intra-abdominal • hand • forearm • elbow • arm • head • neck • trunk • hip • leg • knee • hip • trunk • shoulder • arm • elbow • wrist • hand • fingers • thumb • neck • brow • eye • face • lips • jaw • tongue • swallowing

genitals • toes

One of the best known reflexes is the knee-jerk provoked by a sharp tap on the tendon just below the knee. When the tendon is tapped, a nerve signal is dispatched rapidly to the spinal cord. There, the signal fires two nerves. It not only fires the sensory nerve leading to the brain; it also loops round through the interneuron to fire the motor nerves leading to the thigh muscles and jerk the knee up.

AUTONOMIC NERVES

Reflexes are not the only nerves not under our conscious control from the brain. Running through the spinal cord and branching out all over the body is another important set of nerves. This is not part of the CNS, but an entirely separate system called the autonomic nervous system. The autonomic nervous system automatically controls all the body's internal activities over which we have no influence.

THE SENSORY MAP

The conscious nervous system provides us with very precise information about every sensation on the outside of the body. Whenever we feel a touch on the skin, for instance, we know exactly how hard and where we have been touched. We know how hard from the rate at which nerve signals are transmitted. We know where because the brain has its own built-in sensory map of the body surface.

The brain's sensory map is not a real map. Rather, it is the pattern that nerve signals play upon the sensory cortex—cortex means rind, and the cortex is the wrinkly outer

The brain has its own built-in map of the body in the cortex that identifies where nerve signals are coming from (the sensory cortex, left half) and going to (the motor cortex, right half). Each area of the cortex is proportional to the number of nerve endings in the corresponding part of the body. Hands, feet and face have the largest proportion, which explains the rather weird image of our bodies in the centre.

edges of the brain. Nerve signals from different parts of the body stimulate different parts of the cortex. So we can identify the origin of each nerve signal by the area of the cortex it stimulates. A similar map on another part of the cortex governs the motor nerves and enables us to direct action commands to exactly the right place.

THE BRAIN

The brain's neuronal network is staggeringly complex. There are more than 15,000 million neurons in the brain. And from each one of these neurons extends thousands of minute nerve fibres to link up with thousands of other nerve fibres. So there are literally billions of synapses in the brain, and many billions times more different pathways for nerve signals to travel along.

The neurons are embedded in a microscopic mesh of glial cells. Glial cells outnumber neurons at least ten to one—there are well over one hundred thousand million glial cells in the brain! Their exact function is unclear, though some seem to help form the myelin sheath around larger nerve fibres and others may supply the neurones with nutrients.

All these cells are incredibly demanding on food and oxygen. Although the brain weighs under 1½ kg (3 lbs)—and 85% of this is water—it demands over a quarter of the body's blood supply. If the oxygen supply is ever cut off, the cells of the brain are irreversibly damaged in less than ten seconds. The brain is also very particular about its food, letting only small glucose molecules in through the blood-brain barrier. The barrier is a very fine sieve which helps to protect our most precious asset by keeping out all but the smallest particles.

AREAS OF THE BRAIN

All the brain looks much the same at first. But a closer look reveals a number of distinct regions. Although the mapping of the brain and its functions has barely begun, the particular role of many of these areas can be identified.

In many ways, the layout of the brain echoes its evolution. It has evolved largely by growing outwards from the top of the spinal cord—which is called, logically enough, the brain stem. As it grew

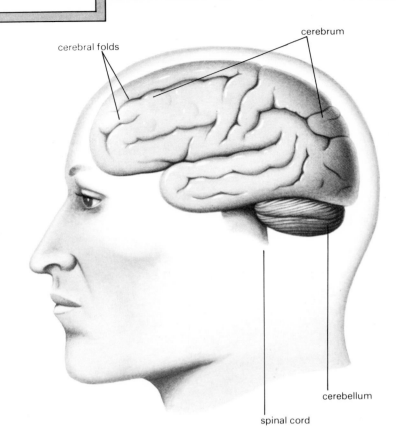

outwards, it became more and more sophisticated. So the cleverer activities—conscious control of movement, speech, and so on—tend to be directed from the outer areas of the brain. The more basic, unconscious activities such as breathing and heart rate are controlled from deeper inside, in the older parts of the brain.

The older, deeper parts of the brain—the hindbrain, the midbrain and the centre of the forebrain—are, in fact, much more varied than the uniform mass of

The two wrinkled grey hemispheres of the brain's cerebrum fill the top of the skull completely. They are folded over and over to squeeze in all the dense network of nerve cells.

grey matter we can see on the outside. Where the spinal cord enters the skull, the bundles of nerves broaden out to form the medulla and the pons. 'Pons' is Latin for bridge, and all nerves must cross this bridge to enter the brain. Between them, the pons and the medulla control many basic bodily

Fact file . . .

There are more than 15,000 million neurons in the brain, each with thousands of synapses.

Girls' brains weigh, on average, 2½ per cent of their body weight (about 1.25 kg, 2½ lbs); boys' brains weigh 2 per cent of their body weight (1.4 kg, 2¾ lbs).

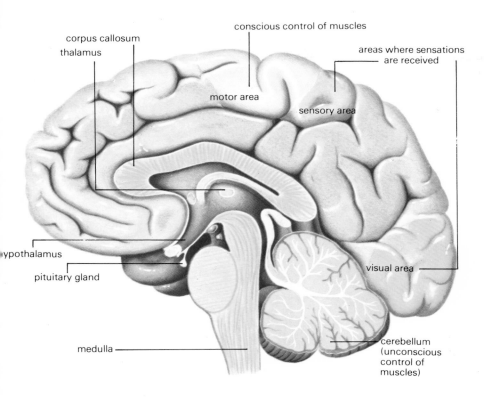

corpus callosum
thalamus
conscious control of muscles
areas where sensations are received
motor area
sensory area
hypothalamus
pituitary gland
visual area
medulla
cerebellum (unconscious control of muscles)

nerve-centre for the autonomic system, regulating everyday activities such as hunger, thirst, temperature, sleeping and waking. It also controls the release of chemical messengers by the pituitary gland (see page 73) and may even influence our emotions, particularly anger and fear. The hypothalamus' companion the thalamus, meanwhile, acts as a relay station for all sensory signals going on into the two huge cerebral hemispheres.

It is in the cerebral hemispheres, occupying almost five-sixths of the brain volume, that most of our brain power lies. It is within its densely packed nerve fibres that we *think*. Here all the conscious sensations such as sight and hearing are felt. Here too are all our deliberate actions decided. And here are contained all our thoughts and basic intelligence. It is in the cerebral hemispheres, if anywhere, that the remarkable human mind is to be found.

Above: This cross-section of the brain shows how it is divided into many distinct regions, each with its own task.

Right: The brain needs an enormous amount of blood to sustain its activity and there is a dense network of capillaries flowing around, but not within, the brain.

functions such as breathing, blood pressure and heart rate.

The third important part of the hindbrain is the cerebellum or little brain. Although it receives all kinds of sensory input, it seems to have no conscious role to play. Its task seems to be the co-ordination of body movements; when the cerebellum is damaged, a person has jerky, badly co-ordinated movements.

In the middle of the giant forebrain is a tiny ball no bigger than the top of your little finger. Despite its small size, this ball, called the hypothalamus, is very important. It not only acts as the

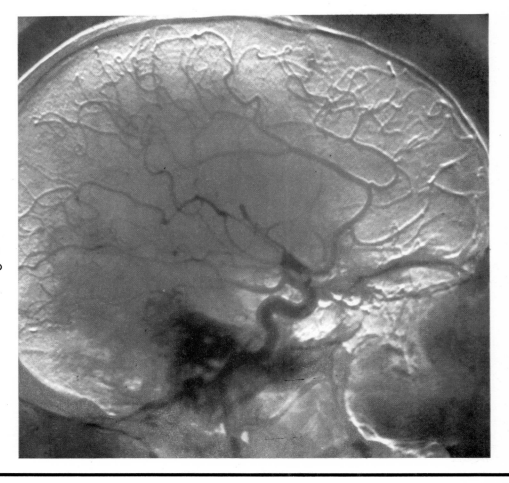

THE HUMAN MIND

The nature of the human mind is a mystery that has puzzled philosophers and scientists for thousands of years. Today, we are still almost as far as ever from understanding how it works—or even just what it is. Yet recent research, helped by radiation-sensitive brain scanners, has demonstrated what scientists have long believed—that many kinds of conscious activity can be linked to particular areas of the cortex.

THE CORTEX

The cortex is the dense mat of grey matter (nerve cell bodies) that forms the rind of the brain, folded over and over to pack as much brain power within the skull as possible. It is split into two halves or hemispheres linked by a knotty bridge of nerve fibres called the corpus callosum. Each hemisphere has the same four lobes: the occipital (at the back), the parietal (on top), the temporal (in the middle, inside the temples) and the frontal. Some regions of the cortex

Left: In the past century, some scientists have attempted to understand the workings of the human mind by examining the way people behave and what they say and feel. Sigmund Freud helped to develop the idea of a subconscious, primitive mind.

Below: Man seems to enjoy exercising his own brain power in intellectually challenging games like chess—a game which involves both the spatially-orientated right brain and the logical left brain.

control conscious movement. Some receive messages from the sense receptors. And others seem to be concerned with language and different kinds of thought from logic and mathematics to artistic ability.

A strip running over the middle of the cortex like the headband from a set of earphones is called the somato-sensory cortex. It is this area of the brain that seems to receive sense messages from all over the body and send out nerve signals to direct conscious movement. Areas linked with other senses are spread around the rest of the cortex, in matching pairs on each of its two halves.

Down at the back, on the occipital lobe, lies the area of the brain associated with sight. Above and to the front, along the top edge of the temporal lobe, is the place where nerve signals from the ears are received. Around both of these areas seem to lie association areas.

INTERPRETING THE SENSES

Links formed with the association areas help us to interpret sensory messages and, literally, make sense of them. Thus in the occipital lobe, for instance, there seem to be areas associated with different visual factors—colour, outline, pattern and other visual criteria. The messages sent by the optic nerves to the brain are like the television signals radiating from the TV mast. Before we can see the TV picture, the signals must be received by the aerial on a TV set and fed through the TV's complex circuitry to create a picture. In the same way, the nerve signal must be received in the visual cortex and fed through the brain's complex circuitry to the association areas to construct the real picture of the world.

In constructing this picture, the brain has to interpret the message —using visual clues, such as outlines and colour—to create real objects out of the jumble of signals from the rods and cones of the eye. On the whole, the brain's interpretative leaps are remarkably accurate. Just occasionally, though, it can be fooled by ambiguous clues (see picture right). This is the basis of all optical illusion.

LANGUAGE AND SPEECH

Besides the senses, the cerebral cortex has areas devoted to language and speech, the most remarkable of all our accomplishments. When people speak, the ear senses waves of sound and feeds nerve signals to the brain. The brain breaks up the stream of sound into words with

Above: Our mental image of food can often over-power the 'real' sensations we feel—a fact that advertisers often play on.

Right: Everything we see is interpreted in the mind — but sometimes the mind can be fooled by ambiguous clues. In this picture, you can sometimes see an old woman, sometimes a young woman.

area. When we speak ourselves, the essence of the message is created in Wernicke's area and then fed forward to Broca's area. Broca's area then co-ordinates the movement of the vocal cords to make the right sounds.

Interestingly, unlike the sense areas which are twinned on either side of the brain, the speech and language centres are only found on the left brain. It seems that the left brain is associated with language and other logical thought processes. The right brain, in contrast, seems to be for artistic, intuitive thought and music. In most people, the link across the corpus callosum seems to ensure that there is a balance between the two, though the left brain is thought to be dominant in most right-handed people.

meaning. Surprisingly, although we hear gaps between words, an analysis of the sound wave shows that there are no such gaps. The brain is actually identifying words and syllables from their context. Just as the eyes can be fooled, so can the ear—it is actually the brain that is fooled in both cases. If a single syllable is replaced in a speech with a mechanical click, the brain interprets the click from its context as the real syllable. People actually hear the missing syllable just as if it is there.

In the brain, an area called Wernicke's area in the temporal lobe seems to be responsible for language, while another area, called Broca's area in the frontal lobe, seems to be responsible for speech. So we interpret what people say to us in Wernicke's

BRAIN WAVES

Sleep is one of the most mysterious of all the body's activities. We spend a good third of our lives sleeping, and a sound night's sleep every 24 hours or so seems to be essential. No-one knows why sleep is so vital. All we know is that the urge to sleep is irresistible.

One of the real problems with understanding sleep is that the bodily differences between sleeping and waking are ambiguous. Heart, breathing and digestion, for instance, carry on almost as if we were awake, though at a slower rate. Even the brain does not shut down altogether. However, some clues to what happens when we sleep come from the brain's electrical activity.

Every neuron produces a small electrical voltage each time it fires. Although it is hard to monitor a single neuron, their combined activity can be recorded on a machine called an electro-encephelograph or EEG.

When we are wide awake, the brain is buzzing with activity. The neurons fire away rapidly, apparently at random, and there is no obvious pattern visible on the EEG. However, as we settle down to sleep and begin to feel drowsy, some of the brain cells begin to fire rhythmically together. The EEG trace shows regular pulses of electrical activity called alpha waves which sweep across the brain every tenth of a second or so accompanied by slower pulses called theta waves. In this state, we are still awake and the fragile rhythm can easily be broken. But, as the EEG traces show, sleep plunges the brain into a regular sequence of activity that is only broken by waking up.

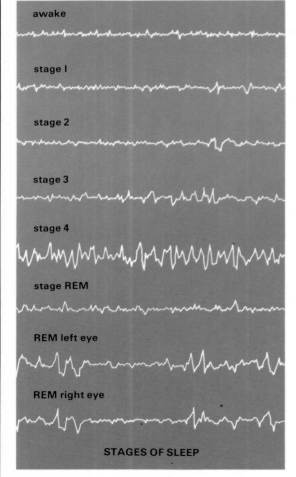

STAGES OF SLEEP

awake

stage 1

stage 2

stage 3

stage 4

stage REM

REM left eye

REM right eye

The different phases of electrical activity in the sleeping brain show clearly on EEG traces (left). We wake when an area of the brain near the pons (below) sends out strong nerve signals that break up the waves of sleep.

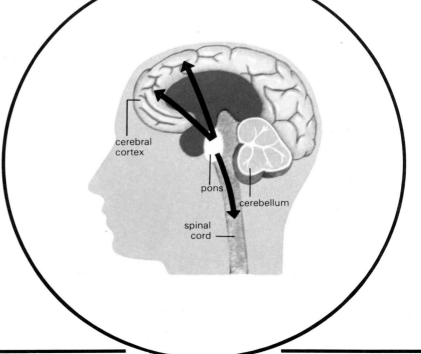

awake

REM sleep (dreams)

drowsiness

slow-wave 'deep' sleep

hours of sleep 0   1

cerebral cortex

pons

cerebellum

spinal cord

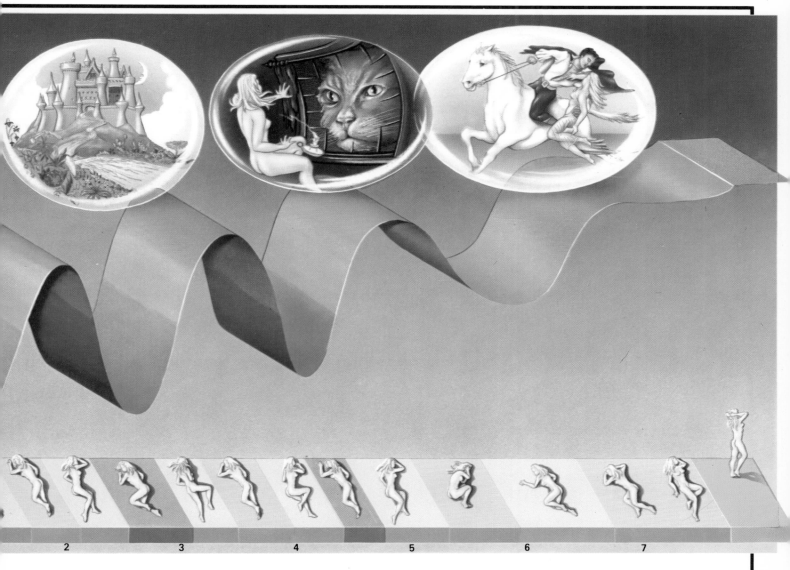

PATTERNS OF SLEEP

Immediately we go to sleep, the breathing steadies and the brain waves begin to become more distinct. This is called Stage 1 sleep. Within a few minutes, Stage 1 gives way to Stage 2 which is marked by stronger slow waves and bursts of rapid waves, called sleep spindles because their trace on the EEG is very spindly.

For the next hour and a half, we fall deeper and deeper into sleep. The slow waves become ever-stronger during Stages 3 and 4, until the entire brain seems to be throbbing gently once or twice a second. The cortex seems to be ticking quietly over preparing for another day.

Then, suddenly, the brain starts to buzz with activity again. Breathing becomes irregular and our bodies begin to move about. Soon, the regular rhythms are swamped out by the random firing of neurons all over the brain. Within minutes, the brain seems to be almost as busy as when we are awake. And yet, strangely, we are harder to rouse than ever.

REM SLEEP

At this stage, the sleeper's eyes begin to flick rapidly from side to side or up and down as if watching. This is called rapid eye movement and active sleep is usually referred to as REM sleep. For the rest of the night, phases of REM sleep lasting half an hour or so alternate with

Throughout the night, phases of deep sleep alternate with the REM sleep that seems to bring our most vivid dreams.

periods of deeper, steadier sleep. These get increasingly shallow and short until finally we wake.

One of the most interesting things about REM sleep is that it seems to be strongly tied in with dreaming. Whenever people are woken directly from REM sleep, they recall vivid dreams. No-one knows exactly why we dream. Some scientists believe it is a time for sorting out the previous day's experience. Others believe it is more significant and reveals truths about our subconscious mind. At the moment, though, the reason remains a mystery.

CO-ORDINATION

Nearly every move we make involves not just one, but a whole sequence of muscle contractions. Even the simplest reflex action, such as pulling a hand away quickly from something hot, demands an intricate set of muscle contractions.

To provide the kind of skillful co-ordination demanded by a pianist or tennis player, the brain must receive a constant stream of information. It must know all the time exactly where each muscle is. If your brain does not know where every part of the body is, you cannot hope to move accurately.

PROPRIOCEPTORS

Information is provided mainly by special sensory nerve endings located in the muscles, tendons, joints and ligaments. These sensors are called proprioceptors. Some kinds of proprioceptors enable you to tell, even with your eyes closed, fairly precisely where every part of the body is. There are also two other types of proprioceptors found in tendons and muscles. These register when the tendon or muscle around them is stretched.

As we make a complex muscular movement, such as hitting a tennis ball, these receptors are firing off signals to the brain. In this way, the brain knows precisely where limbs, tendons and muscles are and exactly how hard each muscle is contracting. Your brain can then return signals to the appropriate muscles to adjust the movement accordingly. As the ball comes towards the racket, for instance, the eye follows it closely. All the while, there is a constant stream of sensory

Hitting a tennis ball demands complex co-ordination by the brain which receives constant information about muscle and limb position, balance and vision. Playing the piano, although a far less strenuous activity, demands an equal amount of co-ordination and control.

signals flowing from the proprioceptors and an equally constant stream of motor signals flowing back from the brain to the muscles of the racket arm. And so all the contractions and relaxations in the muscles can be finely adjusted every fraction of a second.

Adding to the complexity of information pouring into the brain are nerve signals from the body's balance organs.

BALANCE

The main organs of balance lie in the inner ear. Here, in the labyrinthine passages of the vestibule, is a complex structure of three semi-circular canals and a pair of spaces called the saccule and the utricle. Between them, these intricate organs detect the effects of gravity and how the head is moving.

Around the edge of each of these three groups of chambers are tiny hairs connected to nerve receptors. In the semi-circular canals, these hairs project from a little mound into a firm jelly-like tongue called the cupula. In the saccule and utricle the hairs project into a bed of chalky material called otolith.

Movement is detected because, when the head moves, fluid in the chamber lags behind a little and so washes back through the chamber. As the fluid washes the cupula or otolith to or fro, the hairs are pulled

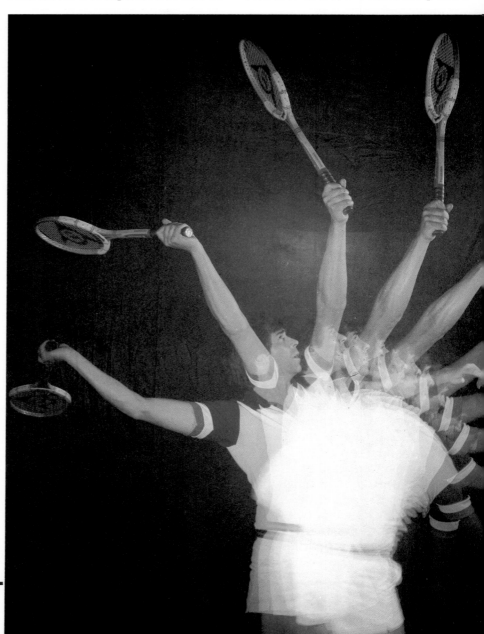

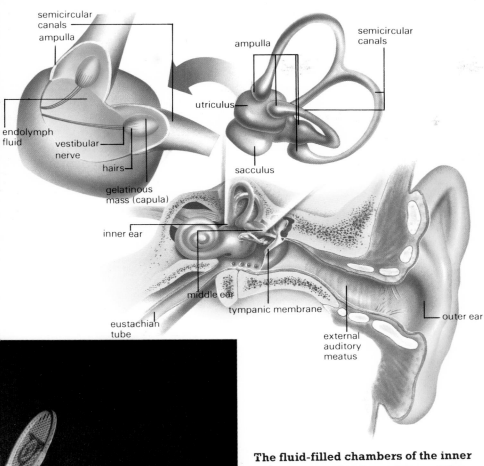

semicircular
canals
ampulla

ampulla

semicircular
canals

utriculus

endolymph
fluid

vestibular
nerve

hairs

sacculus

gelatinous
mass (capula)

inner ear

middle ear

tympanic membrane

eustachian
tube

external
auditory
meatus

outer ear

from side to side. If the hairs are bent in one direction, they send a rapid sequence of signals to the brain. If they are bent in the other direction, the rate of firing decreases.

The hairs in the semi-circular canals are stimulated when you either nod or shake your head. The utricle and saccule react when you tilt your head—or entire body—to one side or the other.

Gravity is detected by the difference in the signals from the utricle and saccule on each side of the head. When the head is level, there is no difference in output, but when your head is on one side, the output on one side decreases while that on the other increases.

All the information from the balance receptors in the ear is fed to the cerebellum at the base of the brain (see page 65). The cerebellum also receives balance information from joint and pressure receptors in the rest of the body—the soles of the feet, for example. This information is then processed in the cerebellum and fed back to the body and on to the cortex of the brain to help co-ordinate movement.

The fluid-filled chambers of the inner ear—the saccule, the utricle and the three semi-circular canals—provide vital information for balance.

HORMONES

Working hand in hand with the nervous system in controlling the body are chemical messengers called hormones. Like nerves, hormones carry signals from one part of the body to another. But while nerves transmit messages in a fraction of a second, hormones are carried in the bloodstream and deliver the message more slowly.

The two systems, nerves and hormones, complement one another well and both are equally vital. Hormones may be much slower to act than nerves, but their effects tend to be more lasting and widespread. So while nerves are used when we need instant results, it is generally hormones that regulate the day-to-day running of the body.

The range of body processes controlled by hormones is vast—not a cell in the body entirely escapes their potent influence. The diagram on the right lists some of the more important hormones and their effects. There are hormones to keep the body working in perfect harmony, such as ADH which helps with water balance. There are hormones like adrenalin that boost the body to peak performance when needed. And there are hormones to regulate our development, such as growth hormones and sex hormones.

Because they produce effects so varied and so dramatic, you might expect hormones to be very distinctive. Yet they are nothing more than tiny chemical molecules,

built up from the same basic ingredients as many other body chemicals. However, each kind of hormone molecule has a particular shape. The shape is crucial, for a hormone's shape is not only its identity card but its message.

Hormones work by changing the internal chemistry of individual cells. To produce the right effect, each hormone must deliver its message to the right series of cells, called its target cells. For some hormones, the target cells may be just one specific type of cell. ADH, for instance, is targeted on the cells of the collecting ducts in the

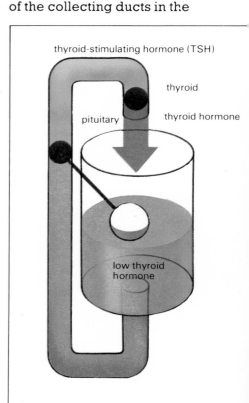

thyroid-stimulating hormone (TSH)

thyroid

pituitary

thyroid hormone

low thyroid hormone

kidneys. Other hormones, such as thyroid hormone, are designed to work on every cell in the body. Each target cell has special receptor sites that can recognize the right hormone by its shape. So as the hormones are washed past in the bloodstream, they slot into the receptors on their target cells like a key into a lock.

The receptors for many larger hormones, such as adrenalin, are on the surface of the cell. As a hormone arrives, a second

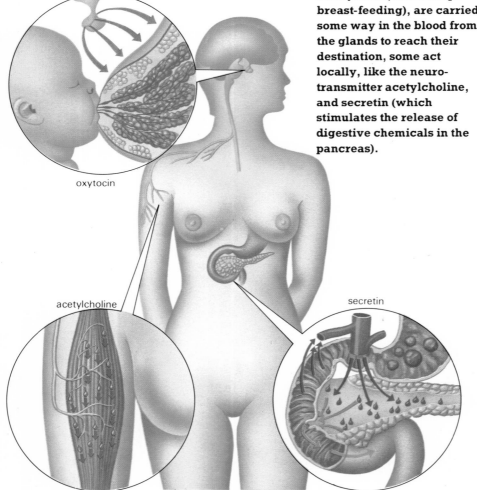

oxytocin

While many hormones, such as oxytocin (which helps breast-feeding), are carried some way in the blood from the glands to reach their destination, some act locally, like the neurotransmitter acetylcholine, and secretin (which stimulates the release of digestive chemicals in the pancreas).

acetylcholine

secretin

Below: The concentration in the blood of hormones that keep things in the body steady—such as temperature and water—must likewise be kept steady by a process called negative feedback. For the thyroid hormone thyroxine, it works like this. The pituitary gland is very sensitive to the amount of thyroxine in the blood. When the level of thyroxine drops too low it releases a substance called thyroid stimulating hormone (TSH). This prods the thyroid to make more thyroxine, thus restoring the level. With the level high once more, the pituitary stops releasing TSH and production of thyroxine ceases.

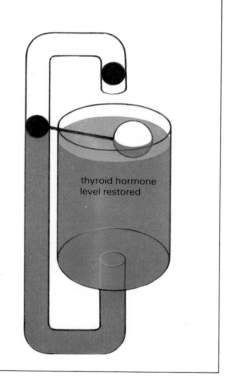

thyroid hormone level restored

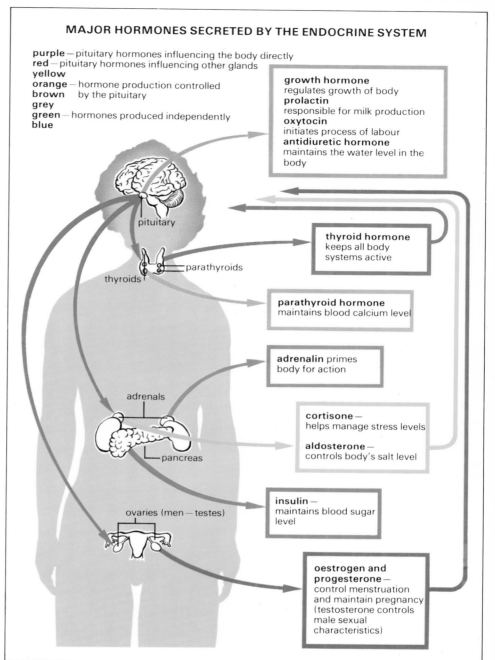

MAJOR HORMONES SECRETED BY THE ENDOCRINE SYSTEM

purple—pituitary hormones influencing the body directly
red—pituitary hormones influencing other glands
yellow
orange—hormone production controlled
brown   by the pituitary
grey
green—hormones produced independently
blue

pituitary

thyroids

parathyroids

adrenals

pancreas

ovaries (men—testes)

growth hormone
regulates growth of body
prolactin
responsible for milk production
oxytocin
initiates process of labour
antidiuretic hormone
maintains the water level in the body

thyroid hormone
keeps all body systems active

parathyroid hormone
maintains blood calcium level

adrenalin primes body for action

cortisone—
helps manage stress levels

aldosterone—
controls body's salt level

insulin—
maintains blood sugar level

oestrogen and progesterone—
control menstruation and maintain pregnancy (testosterone controls male sexual characteristics)

chemical messenger—typically cyclic AMP—sets off inside the cell to pass on the news to the chemical that will set events in motion. It is as if the hormone is the postman, delivering a letter to the front door, while cyclic AMP is the receptionist taking the letter in to the foreman of the works. Many smaller hormone molecules such as the thyroid hormones, however, are able to slip through the cell walls and link up with receptors floating inside the cell.

ENDOCRINE GLANDS

Many of the body's hormones are made in special glands next to major blood vessels. These glands are called endocrine glands, and hormone control is often known as the endocrine system.

Each gland secretes a different set of hormones and so controls different body processes. The thyroid gland in the neck, for instance, controls how fast we burn our food with its hormone thyroxine. The nearby parathyroid gland secretes a hormone that balances levels of calcium in the body.

In many ways, though, it is the pituitary gland that is the key to the whole system. This tiny, pea-sized gland in the head sends out a range of hormones just like any other gland. But it also releases special tropic hormones that co-ordinate the release of hormones from many other glands.

HORMONES AT WORK

Of all the body's hormones, adrenalin and insulin are perhaps the best known. Adrenalin's effect is so powerful and dramatic that we can actually feel it in action. Indeed, feeling 'a surge of adrenalin' is part of our everyday language. The effects of insulin are equally dramatic—but only if things go wrong. Without enough insulin in the bloodstream, we suffer from the illness diabetes.

THE POWER OF FEAR

Adrenalin is part of the body's emergency action team. Whenever danger threatens, the body reacts in a number of ways. If you have ever been in a car that has narrowly avoided an accident, you probably remember some of these reactions.

Our first response to danger is, literally, a nervous one. The nerves send messages to the brain warning of the danger. The brain instantly

Whenever danger threatens, the adrenal glands on top of the kidneys secrete adrenalin, a hormone that boosts all the body systems ready for action.

galvanizes the body into action to avert the threat. A rapid burst of nerve impulses to the appropriate muscles makes us duck, cover our head, jump out of the way, or whatever seems to be the safest course. But at the same time, the brain sends out an instant alarm to a pair of endocrine glands nestling on top of the kidneys. These glands are called the adrenals, which simple means above (ad-) the kidneys (renal).

Each of the adrenal glands has two distinct parts. There is the cortex which, like the cortex of the brain, is the outer part, the rind of the gland. And there is the medulla which is the inner core. Each part secretes, among other hormones, three hormones that play a major part in the body's response to danger. Two of these hormones, adrenalin and noradrenalin, come from the medulla; the other, cortisol, comes from the cortex.

When the alarm call arrives from the brain, the medulla releases a flood of adrenalin and noradrenalin into the bloodstream. Within seconds, the two hormones are binding on to target cells throughout the body. Indeed some of the effects are so rapid that we scarcely notice any delay between sensing the danger and feeling the effects of adrenalin.

FIGHT OR FLIGHT

What adrenalin and noradrenalin do is prepare the body for emergency action. We can escape from most tricky situations either by standing to face the threat or by running away. So the effects of the two hormones are often called the body's 'fight or flight' response.

In essence, adrenalin and noradrenalin prepare the body for action in three ways. They boost the supply of oxygen and energy-giving glucose to the muscles that we will need to fight or run away; they shut down body processes that might be distracting; and they generally make us more alert.

Almost the instant adrenalin and noradrenalin pour into the blood, the heart begins to beat stronger and faster to boost the blood supply. Blood vessels in the muscles widen while others narrow, channelling blood to the muscles where it is needed. Breathing deepens and quickens to increase oxygen intake. And the liver breaks down its stores of glycogen to release more glucose into the blood.

Besides these dramatic internal changes, the two hormones have a number of effects visible on the outside. Eyes widen to help us see better, hair stands on end, and our skin goes pale and cold as the blood supply is reduced. We may even start to sweat to keep our increasingly active body cool.

Meanwhile, as adrenalin and noradrenalin are preparing us for action, a hormone from the pituitary gland triggers off the release of cortisol from the adrenal cortex.

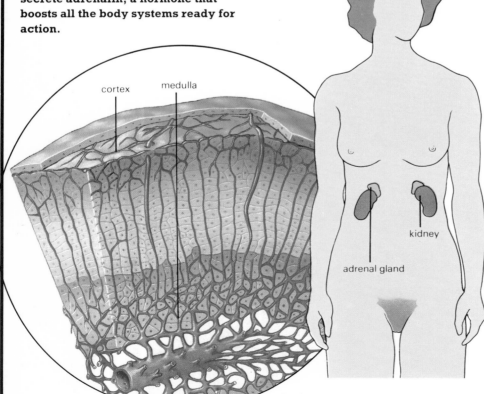

cortex   medulla

kidney

adrenal gland

Cortisol is slower to work, but it helps the body to cope with the possible consequences of danger. It unlocks the energy lying dormant as fat; it mobilizes amino acids to aid repair work since we may be injured; and it helps to reduce pain. Cortisol is actually so effective in reducing pain that people are often unaware of an injury until after the danger has passed and the levels of cortisol drop.

BLOOD SUGAR

Insulin plays a vital role in keeping the levels of glucose (sugar) in the blood under control. It not only helps turn glucose into glycogen in the liver, it also helps the body's cells draw glucose out of the blood

to use as energy. In this way it prevents the level of glucose in the blood ever rising too high.

Insulin is produced by small groups of cells within the pancreas, known as the islets of Langerhans. Besides insulin, these cells produce another hormone, called glucagon. Glucagon has exactly the opposite effect to insulin, boosting the blood sugar by speeding up the breakdown of glycogen in the liver.

Between them insulin and glucagon ensure that the blood sugar level is always just right. If the blood sugar level drops, the pancreas releases more glucagon to make up the loss; if it rises too high, the pancreas releases more insulin.

Unfortunately, in some people, the pancreas sometimes fails to produce enough insulin, a problem known as diabetes. Without insulin, glucose cannot get into the body cells and the blood sugar level rises. Some sugar escapes through the kidneys in the urine. But as it does so, it drags body water with it—one of the first signs of diabetes is extreme thirst. Worse still, the body's cells, starved of glucose turn to fats and proteins for energy, causing muscle wasting and a build-up of poisonous ketone bodies. At present, the only solutions are tablets or regular injections of insulin.

Right: The body reacts to the thrill of a rollercoaster ride by calling adrenalin into action. It is perhaps the stimulating effects of adrenalin that make fear so much fun.

Below: Whenever the level of glucose in the blood rises too high, the pancreas secretes more insulin, which increases the amount of glucose stored in the liver, and speeds movement of glucose from the blood into the body cells.

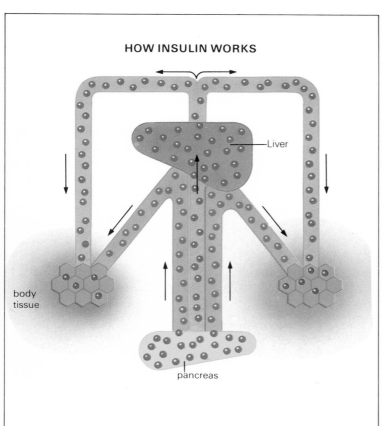

HOW INSULIN WORKS

Liver

body tissue

pancreas

BODY HEAT

Sometimes the world we live in is baking hot; sometimes it is freezing cold. Yet within our bodies the temperature remains forever the same, rarely dropping more than a few degrees below 37°C (98.6°F), nor rising more than a few degrees above.

This thermographic image shows how the body maintains a warm core while losing heat through the skin to cold air and surfaces.

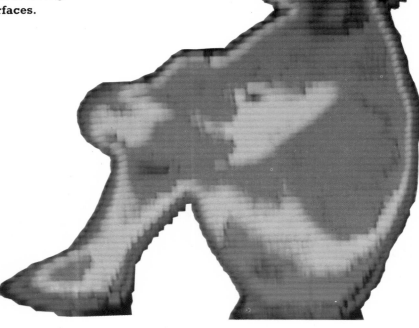

The body needs this steady temperature to ensure that all the chemical reactions work properly. Wide fluctuations in temperature would not only upset the delicate balance between the various processes; it might stop some working altogether. Some parts of the body, such as the brain and the internal organs, are particularly sensitive to heat and cold. Others, such as the feet, may be a good 10°C or more colder without suffering unduly. So the body concentrates on maintaining a rock steady core temperature while tolerating a little variation at the extremities. It does this by a very simple process: it creates heat when it is cool and loses heat as it warms up.

Most of our body heat comes from the continual burning of food in every cell. Indeed, nearly all the food we eat is turned into heat. Some of this heat comes from the non-stop chemical activity of the internal organs, especially the liver. Some comes from the turmoil of digestion. But by far the majority comes from the incessant motion of muscle. Indeed, when we're working hard, the muscles can produce as much heat as a two bar electric fire.

Even at rest, our bodies generate so much heat that we are only comfortable when the air is somewhat cooler than the body. Only if the air is cooler can we lose this excess heat easily. Then we can lose heat simply by breathing. But more significantly, our bodies lose heat through the skin.

With the air temperature about 12°C (20°F) cooler, the heat we create is roughly balanced by the heat we lose. So the core temperature stays steady very easily. Living in warm houses and wearing warm clothes helps to insulate us from any changes in the air temperature. Sometimes, however, the air surrounding the body may get too cold or too hot for this easy balance to be maintained. When this happens, the body must take more positive action.

Below: When we are hot, arterioles in the skin dilate to help heat escape from the body quickly, and sweat increases to cool us by evaporation.

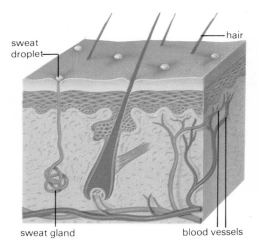

Below: When we are cold, the blood vessels constrict to cut down heat loss, and hairs stand on end, pulled upright by erector muscles connected to the hair follicles. This is a hangover from the days of our more hairy ancestors.

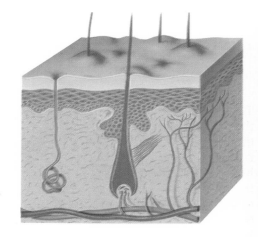

The hypothalamus receives information about the body's temperature in two ways: the heat of the blood passing through it and the messages from the temperature sensitive nerve endings.

The body is equipped with a range of automatic heating and cooling mechanisms to help us keep body temperature completely steady.

The cold sensors fire off nerve signals rapidly when the skin is cold but slowly when it warms up; the warm sensors fire rapidly when it is warm. And finally there are sensors in the all important core of the body, perhaps in the central nervous system. So the hypothalamus gets a good overall picture of body temperature by comparing the skin and core temperatures with its own blood temperature measurements.

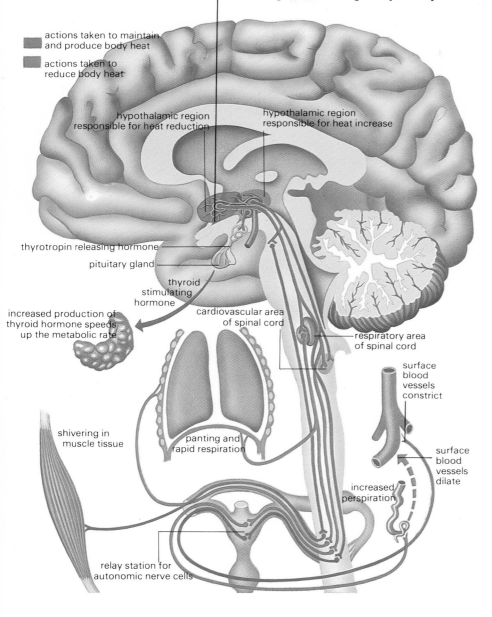

actions taken to maintain and produce body heat

actions taken to reduce body heat

hypothalamic region responsible for heat reduction

hypothalamic region responsible for heat increase

thyrotropin releasing hormone

pituitary gland

thyroid stimulating hormone

increased production of thyroid hormone speeds up the metabolic rate

cardiovascular area of spinal cord

respiratory area of spinal cord

surface blood vessels constrict

shivering in muscle tissue

panting and rapid respiration

surface blood vessels dilate

increased perspiration

relay station for autonomic nerve cells

HOT AND COLD

If the body seems to be getting cold, we take a number of conscious actions to keep warm, such as putting on more clothes, turning on the fire and running about to generate muscle heat. But under the direction of the hypothalamus the body takes a number of less obvious steps to keep warm. Blood vessels in the skin begin to constrict to keep blood snugly in the core. Less usefully, tiny muscles pull erect the tiny hairs in the skin, forming goose pimples. This is probably a remnant from our ancestors who had very hairy bodies—raising the hairs trapped a layer of warm air above the skin. And we begin to shiver, as muscles all over the body go into a rapid little series of contractions to generate heat.

When the body gets too warm, a similar mixture of conscious and unconscious actions helps us to cool down. While we open the window or remove a jumper, the hypothalamus is also at work. Blood vessels in the skin widen to carry more heat away through the skin. And we start to sweat, as water is exuded through sweat glands all over the skin. Sweating not only takes warm water out of the body, it also cools the skin by evaporating. Evaporation, changing from liquid to vapour, needs energy and the energy for evaporation from the skin is the heat from local blood vessels. So as sweat evaporates, it takes heat from the body away with it.

THERMOSTATIC CONTROL

The key to temperature control in the body is the 'hypothalamus', a tiny but vital tangle of nerve cells right in the centre of the brain. The hypothalamus is the body's own thermostat, programmed from birth to keep the body at the right temperature. If the body is too warm or too cold, the hypothalamus

sends out signals to heating and cooling mechanisms around the body. But to perform its task, the hypothalamus must receive a constant stream of information from various temperature sensors.

There are basically three types of sensor. First of all, there are sensors in the hypothalamus itself that measure the temperature of the blood flowing around it. Then there are sensors in the skin, some sensitive to cold and some to heat.

CHAPTER 5

BLUEPRINT FOR LIFE

Human DNA is the chemical blueprint that makes each individual a unique person. A person's DNA comes equally from his or her mother and father, and determines all processes of development from the fertilized egg to full maturity, and all features of the growing and mature body. DNA itself, in the nuclei of our body cells, is built up of chemical units that the body reads as a 'genetic code'.

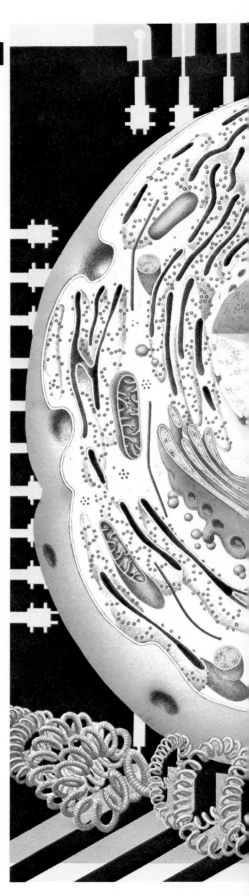

Each cell of the body, though linked to and reliant on the other cells of the body in a wide variety of ways, contains complete instructions to make an entire body in the form of a chemical called 'DNA'.

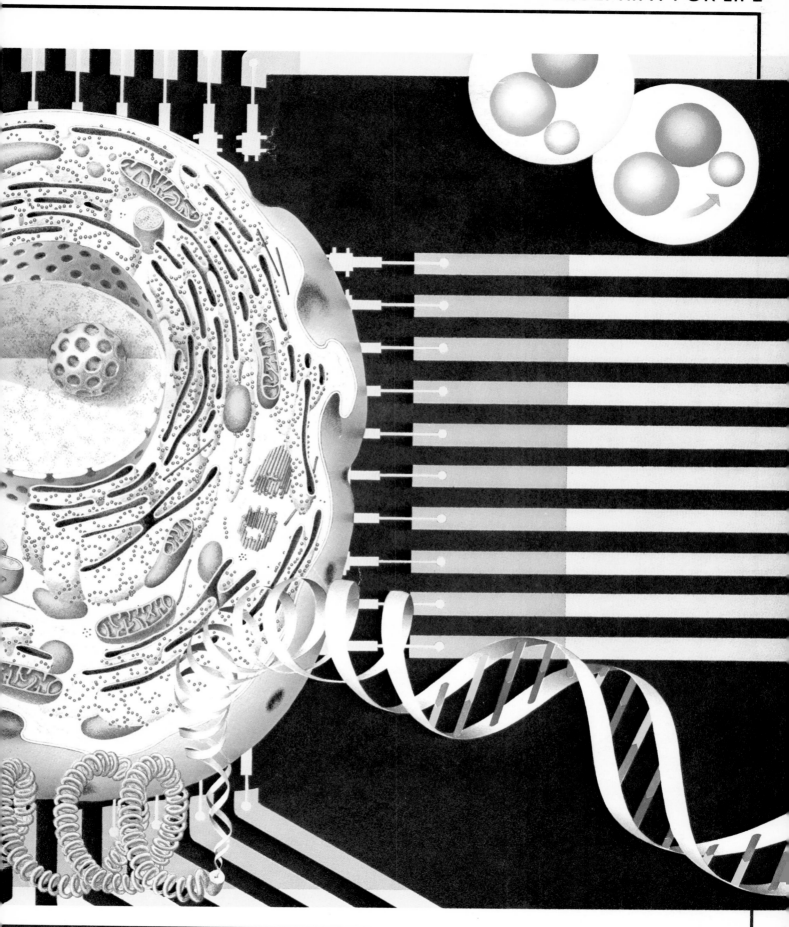

THE GENETIC CODE

Within every cell in the body is a remarkable molecule, a molecule so important that it is often described as the chemical basis of life. Called deoxyribonucleic acid, or DNA for short, this molecule contains an enormous amount of information—there is enough information stored in DNA in each cell to fill a library of 3000 books or the memory of over 85,000 64K home computers. In coded form, the DNA in each cell carries the instructions to make an exact copy not merely of the cell but of your entire body.

Naturally, the DNA molecule is large. In fact, it is one of the largest molecules known to man. It is not very wide but enormously long. When stretched out, it would be over 5 cm (2 in) long.

Below: The sequence of bases running down each of the twin spiral strands of the DNA molecule are the key to the body's genetic code.

When this giant molecule was finally unravelled, barely 30 years ago, it was found to contain not one, but two strands, wrapped tightly round each other in a long spiral called a double helix—helix just means spiral. In a way, the DNA molecule is rather like an incredibly long, twisted ladder. The sides of the ladder are strands of chemical building blocks called bases, 240 million long, strung together like beads on a necklace. The rungs of the ladder are special chemical bonds called hydrogen bonds that link pairs of bases.

There are four kinds of bases in the DNA strand: two large bases, guanine and adenine (G and A); and two small ones, cytosine and thymine (C and T). These bases are very choosy about what they will pair with in hydrogen bonds. Guanine only pairs with cytosine (and vice versa), and adenine only pairs with thymine (and vice versa). This is important, for it means that the arrangement of bases along one strand of the DNA molecule precisely mirrors that in the other. One is, if you like, a negative copy of the other.

GENES

The key to the DNA's code lies in the order in which the four bases are strung together along each strand. Each base is like a letter of the alphabet, and the sequence of bases along the DNA strand is put together in chunks of instructions like sentences. These sentences are called genes.

A gene is basically the cell's instructions for building a protein,

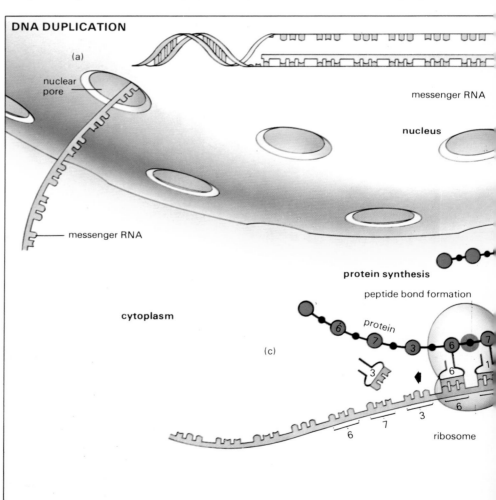

DNA DUPLICATION

(a)

nuclear pore

messenger RNA

messenger RNA

nucleus

cytoplasm

(c)

protein synthesis

peptide bond formation

protein

ribosome

Below: A strand of DNA magnified many times (left) and (right) a model of the intricate double helix structure of the molecule which was first worked out by Watson and Crick in the early 1950s.

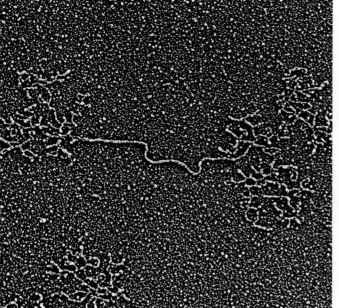

acids, some codons code for the same amino acids, and three codons are reserved as 'full stops' to mark the end of each gene sequence.

PROTEIN BUILDING

All the amino acids needed are ready on hand within the cell to build up proteins according to instructions. But the DNA is too valuable to use directly as a mould. And the cell very rarely wants to use more than a tiny sentence of the DNA's thousands of books-worth of instructions. So the DNA is stowed safely inside the nucleus. When the cell needs the instructions to make a certain protein, it sends a special enzyme to get a copy of the genes wanted.

The copies of DNA are made in the form of molecules of another chemical, called RNA. RNA is like DNA but has only one strand rather than two. When instructed by the enzyme, the DNA strand will temporarily split at the appropriate point and the RNA will match up with the exposed sequence of bases to make a perfect imprint. This imprinted copy is called messenger RNA or mRNA.

When the mRNA enters the cytoplasm it links up with a ribosome. Elsewhere in the cytoplasm, another type of RNA, called transfer RNA or tRNA is gathering the ingredients. tRNA is very short, just one codon long, and has a special hook for the amino acid it codes for. Hooking the right amino acid, the tRNA moves towards the line of mRNA and links up matching codons on the mRNA.

The strand of mRNA feeds through the ribosome like a tape past the playback head of a tape recorder. As it feeds through, the ribosome knits together the amino acids hooked on the end of the tRNA, codon by codon, binding them in a long chain corresponding to the sequence encoded on the mRNA. In this way, a protein is made precisely according to the instructions in the DNA molecule.

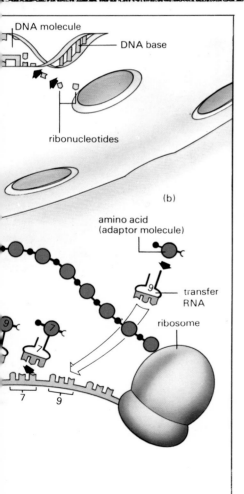

Left: The instructions for making anything from individual protein molecules to our entire bodies are coded in the giant DNA molecule in the nucleus of every cell. This is never used as a mould directly, but copied into short strands of messenger RNA. And proteins are synthesized (assembled) in the cytoplasm of the cell as the ribosome runs along the strand of mRNA knitting together the amino acids gathered by tRNA.

which can either be structural or an enzyme. Each protein is constructed from different combinations of 20 amino acids—the protein's building blocks. So to code for a particular protein, the gene must specify which amino acids are to be used. This is where the sequence of bases comes in.

Like letters, the individual bases only mean something when combined to form a word. In DNA, each word, called a codon, is a combination of three of the four bases. Each codon 'means' one particular amino acid. Altogether, there are 64 different ways in which three of a possible four bases can be combined, and so 64 codons exist. But as there are only 20 amino

CELL REGENERATION

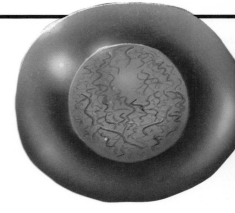

Few cells can go on working perfectly forever. Sooner or later, they must be replaced. Fortunatley, cells all over the body are continually dividing and re-dividing to create new cells.

When cells divide, the daughter cells must not only look the same as the parent; they must receive an identical set of genetic instructions. So before each cell divides, it makes a copy of its DNA. It can then pass on one copy to each of the daughter cells.

Although the structure of DNA is enormously complex, the cell manages to copy the whole sequence quickly and, usually, with complete accuracy. This process is called replication. What happens is that the double strands of the DNA molecule gradually unzip, exposing the mirror image sequences of bases. Bases floating freely within the nucleus of the cell, called free bases, soon find their chosen partners in the exposed strands, adenine linking up with thymine bases and guanine with cytosine. As the free bases slot into place on one of the DNA strands they are bonded together in exactly the same order as the other DNA

As a cell divides by mitosis, the tangle of chromosomes (below) is slowly unravelled (below centre) and split in half (below right) to give each daughter cell an identical genetic blueprint.

strand. The same thing happens on the other strand. So two identical copies of DNA are formed.

DNA does not just float freely in the cell nucleus. It is combined with protein to form long, knotted skeins called chromosomes. Chromosomes are, like genes, basic genetic units. But if the genes carry a sentence of information, each chromosome carries an entire book.

MITOSIS

While DNA is being copied, the structure of the chromosome is vague. But as the cell begins to divide, the chromosomes become more distinct. Their thread-like appearance at this stage gives this process of cell division its name mitosis, from the Greek word mitos meaning thread. Soon it becomes clear that each chromosome is not a single thread but two, joined together by a centromere which ties them together like the knot in a bow tie. These two threads carry identical genetic information, copied by DNA replication. During mitosis, the knot holding them together loosens and one thread goes to each daughter cell. So each daughter cell ends up with an identical set of chromosomes.

As the chromosomes split, they are drawn towards opposite ends of the dividing cell along fine spindly threads of protein. Soon they cluster

so tightly at each end of the elongated cell that they appear as dark balls. An inner membrane forms around each ball and the waist of the cell begins to narrow. Finally, an outer membrane forms across the waist to create two identical new cells.

MEIOSIS

Mitosis is quite adequate for all the billions of cell divisions during our lifetime. But before we are even conceived, a different process of cell division, called meiosis, must occur.

In every cell in your body, there are two sets of chromosomes, one inherited from your mother and the other from your father. Because there are two sets, these cells are called diploid cells. For a new human being to be created, it too must receive chromosomes from each of its parents. But if every new human had two sets from each parent—that is, four sets—the cell would soon be overcrowded with information, most of it unnecessary.

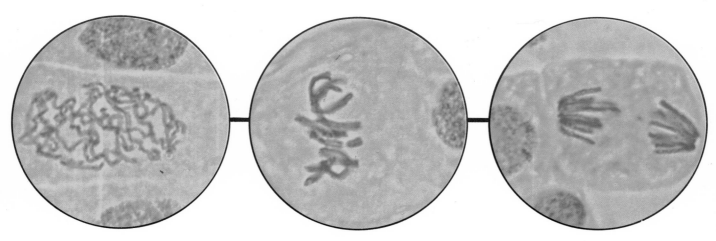

Cell division by meiosis creates sex cells with half the normal number of chromosomes. Normally, the threads of individual chromosome are barely visible in the cell nucleus (above left).

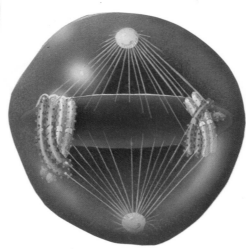

As meiosis begins, chromosomes inherited from the father pair up with corresponding chromosomes inherited from the mother (left) and each duplicates itself. They then swap genetic material and line up along the middle of the cell (below).

The answer to this problem lies in the sex cells or gametes. The sex cells—eggs and sperm—are the cells from each parent that combine to make a new human being. They have exactly half the number of chromosomes that every other cell in the body has, and are called haploid cells. So when sex cells from each parent combine, the resulting cells have not four sets of chromosomes but two.

It is through the process of meiosis that the number of chromosomes in each cell is halved. Meiosis has two stages following on closely. In the first stage, the chromosomes pair up and, in a process called crossing-over, swap a portion of genetic material. This ensures that each new cell has a mixture of genes from both parents. Next, the cell divides, distributing one chromosome from each pair to each of the daughter cells. In the second stage, the two new cells divide again as in mitosis with half of each chromosome going to each of the four daughter cells.

nucleotide base pairs

original DNA strand

new nucleotide bases joining

new DNA strand

Above: To make copies of the genetic material encoded in DNA, the two strands of DNA unzip so that free floating bases can latch on to the exposed strands, forming two entirely new strands.

As the cell divides, half the pairs of chromosomes go to each new cell bud (above). But as the cell starts to divide (right), it splits the other way as well, creating four new cells and splitting the chromosome pairs into single strands.

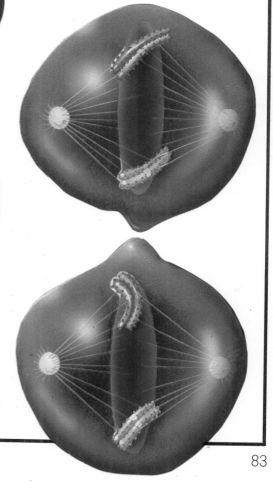

HEREDITY

Nearly everyone resembles their parents to some extent. Indeed, so thoroughly reliable is the genetic blueprint passed on from parents to children that we are surprised if they don't. And yet no two human beings, out of more than 4000 million in the world, are exactly alike.

This marvellous balance between precision and waywardness in our inherited characteristics stems largely from our chromosomes. There are 46 chromosomes in every human cell (except for the sex cell). And, as we have just seen, these 46 chromosomes can be arranged into pairs. In women, the chromosomes match up into 23 pairs. In men, though, there are only 22 matching pairs and two odd chromosomes.

SEX CELLS

The odd chromosomes in men are the sex chromosomes which are called X and Y because of their shape. A woman also has sex chromosomes in her cells, but hers are a matching pair of Xs. The sex chromosomes determine whether a baby will be a boy or a girl. The

Below: Parents with brown eyes may have children with blue eyes if they carry recessive genes for this characteristic. But the child must inherit the recessive gene from both parents. Three out of four times, the child will receive the dominant genes from one or both parents and have brown eyes. Blond hair and small noses can be inherited in the same way (bottom). Often, though, there is more than one gene involved and there is a variety of possible combinations (polygene inheritance).

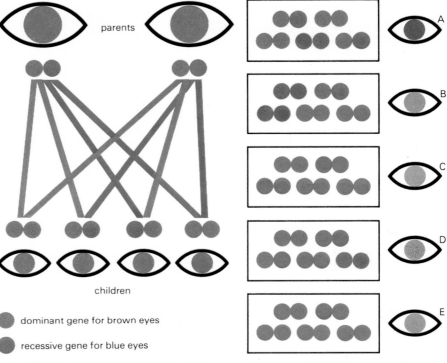

single-factor inheritance

parents

children

- dominant gene for brown eyes
- recessive gene for blue eyes

polygene inheritance

children

A B C D E

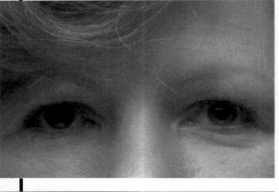

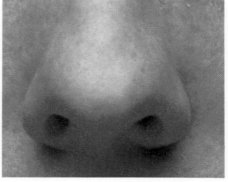

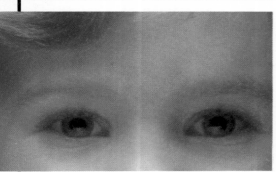

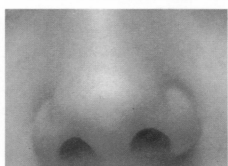

Right: Twins have played a major role in our understanding of heredity, because they have a similar genetic background. However, most twins come from different eggs (fraternal twins) and have slightly different genes. Only identical twins (right) who came originally from the same egg have exactly the same genetic make-up.

determining factor is where the sex chromosomes go when the cells divide during meiosis. In a woman, who has two X chromosomes, the sex cell will always get an X chromosome. But in a man, who has an X and a Y, half the sex cells get an X and half a Y. So during fertilization (see page 95), the woman's sex cell may combine with a man's sex cell containing either an X chromosome or a Y. If it combines with an X, the baby will be a girl; if it combines with a Y, it will be a boy.

MECHANISMS OF INHERITANCE

Apart from the sex chromosomes, all the other 44 chromosomes always come in pairs. In every pair, both chromosomes probably provide instructions for the same things. And the same features seem to be coded for by genes in the same place on each paired chromosome, a place called a gene locus. So we have two alternative sets of instructions for each feature.

Much of the time, the result will be a mixture of the two. Sometimes, however, there can be no compromise; either one or the other gene must win. A gene that always wins is called a dominant gene; a gene that loses is called a recessive gene. Although the recessive gene loses out in battle with the dominant, it does make its presence felt when it is paired with another recessive gene.

Brown eyes are often coded by a gene which is dominant over a gene for blue eyes. Two parents,

fraternal twins — separate eggs — polar body — identical twins — single egg fertilized by single sperm — separate sperms — 2-cell stage zygotes — 2-cell stage zygote — amniotic cavity

both with brown eyes, may carry both sets of genes, even though the dominant brown eye gene is expressed. If they have four children, the chances are that three will have brown eyes because they inherit the dominant brown eye gene from either one or both parents. One of the children, however, may inherit the recessive gene from both parents. In this case the blue eye gene, freed from competition, will express itself and the child has blue eyes.

Such an example shows genes clearly in action. But most of our inherited features are not so easy to follow through generations. One complication is that each chromosome may carry many genes, called polygenes, to specify a single feature. So the number of possible combinations between the polygenes of both chromosomes is very large. An added complication is crossing-over, when genes are swapped between chromosomes during meiosis.

MISPRINTS

Every now and then, the almost perfectly reliable genetic code makes a slip. Sometimes, it gets just a single base wrong in a sequence of many millions. Sometimes, it misses by an entire chromosome. These mistakes are called mutations and the chromosome or gene at fault is a mutant.

Genes mutate when DNA is copied wrongly before a cell divides. Exposure to certain chemicals and radiation increases the mutation rate. But many mutations seem to occur at random.

Because the mutant gene is a recessive gene on the X chromosome (Xc), red-green colour-blindness is inherited on a sex-linked basis (below).

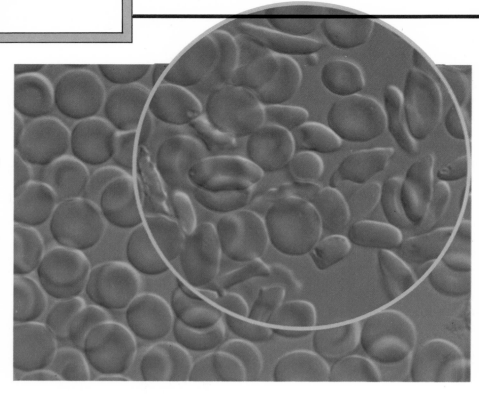

Above: A mutation of a single base in the genes for haemoglobin causes the disease called sickle-cell anaemia with its distinctive sickle-shaped red blood cells.

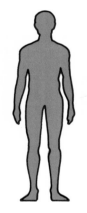   

colour-blind male	normal female		colour-blind male	female carrier
XcY	XX		XcY	XcX

 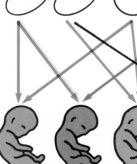

| XcX female carrier | XcX female carrier | XY normal male | XY normal male | XcX female carrier | XcXc colour-blind female | XY normal male | XcY colour-blind male |

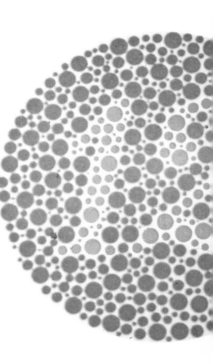

Gene mutations may well have played a key role in our evolution. Mutations seem to be the main way —perhaps the only way—we can acquire completely new characteristics. Because they involve changes to the genetic code, they can be passed on to future generations. One theory of evolution is, very simply, that mutations which increased a mutant's chances of surviving and breeding are passed on—because the mutant survives and has offspring to pass the mutation on to. Mutations that reduce the chances of survival tend to die out.

SICKLE-CELL ANAEMIA

Not all mutations that have a bad rather than good effect die out, however. If the person carrying the mutant gene lives long enough to have children, even a bad gene may be passed on for many generations. Because such bad genes tend to stand out, more is known about mutations that cause problems than those that do good.

One of the best known inherited mutant genes is a fault in the gene coding for haemoglobin (see page 15). Haemoglobin is the pigment in red blood cells that carries oxygen through the blood. In a person suffering from sickle-cell anaemia, the DNA codes for the wrong form of haemoglobin. This haemoglobin, called sickle-cell haemoglobin (Hbs), tends not to dissolve well when deprived of oxygen. So when there is little oxygen in the blood, Hbs crystallizes into long fibres that stretch the blood cells into the characteristic sickle shape. These cells are quickly broken up and the person becomes anaemic (short of red blood cells). The fault seems to lie with a single base out of all the hundreds coding for the amino acids that create haemoglobin. But this single slip is quite enough to change the nature of haemoglobin completely.

Interestingly, sickle-cell anaemia is very common in Africa in precisely the same areas as malaria. The sickle-cell anaemia gene seems to protect people from malaria in some way. So those who possess the sickle-cell gene have a better chance of surviving and passing on the mutant gene.

COLOUR BLINDNESS

Sometimes, gene mutations can occur on the sex chromosomes. If this happens, a fault can be inherited in an intricate sex-linked pattern. A form of colour-blindness that makes people unable to distinguish between red and green follows this pattern.

The gene for red-green colour-blindness is a recessive gene on the X chromosome. If a woman has this on one of her two X chromosomes, it will be over-ridden by the normal gene on the other. So she is not colour blind. A man, however, has only one X chromosome, so a mutant gene on the X chromosome will make him colour-blind.

A woman carrying the gene may pass it on to some of her children. But only the boys who are unlucky enough to get the chromosome carrying the gene will be colour-blind. Girls still have their father's normal gene to fall back on. The only time a woman will suffer from this kind of colour-blindness is if she receives a mutant gene from each of her parents.

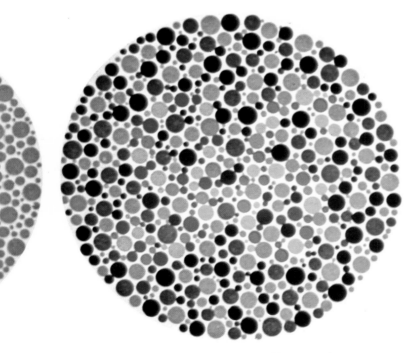

Above: People who inherit the gene for colour-blindness are unable to identify both numbers picked out in dots above.

Right: Very rarely, gene mutation may cause extreme differences in growth, such as giants and dwarfs.

CHAPTER 6

HUMAN LIFE

Sex and reproduction are more dramatic processes in human beings than in the vast majority of other animals. We are much slower to mature than most animals but our sexual behaviour is more complex because it is largely a product of our extra-large brain. Human pregnancy and birth, and the long period of human mothering, are also characteristically complex parts of our lives.

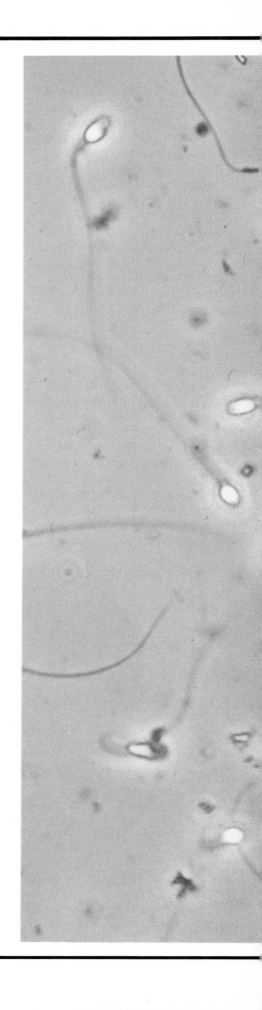

New human babies can only be formed by the mating of one of these tiny human sperm, produced by a man, and an ova (egg) in a woman's womb.

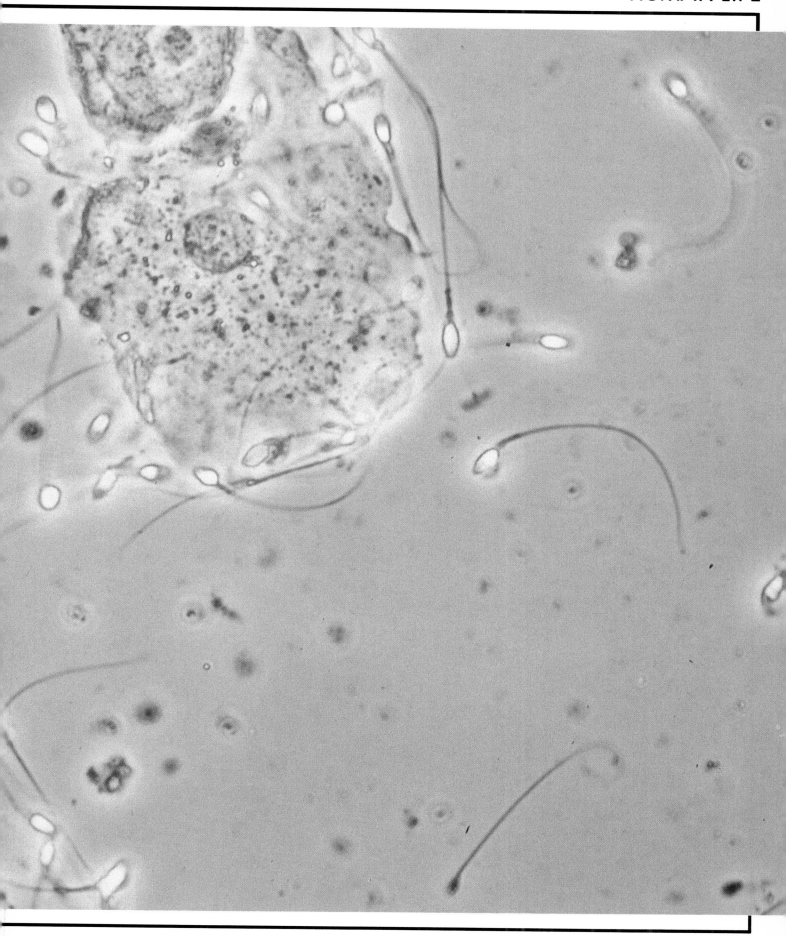

PUBERTY

At the age of eleven years or so, your body begins to change with a speed it has rarely done before or will ever do again. Almost overnight, your body is transformed subtly from a child's to an adult's. Girls begin to become women and boys to become men.

These momentous changes affect the whole of your body and personality, but they are rooted in developing sexual identity. From the onset of puberty, your body undergoes physical changes that will enable you to have sex and create new human beings. And at the same time, you become increasingly aware of your own sexuality.

SEX HORMONES

No-one knows quite what triggers off these changes. But they depend on rising levels in the blood of two hormones, follicle stimulating hormone (FSH) and luteinizing hormone (LH). These hormones both come from the pituitary gland (see page 73). Since the pituitary gland is controlled by the small tangle of nerves in the brain called the hypothalamus the answer seems to lie in the hypothalamus. Some scientists believe that during childhood the hypothalamus keeps the levels of FSH and LH in check, only letting them rise at puberty. Others believe that the hypothalamus only grows the right nerves to stimulate the pituitary to release FSH and LH when you reach puberty.

When the levels of FSH and LH start to climb, they spark off a rapid growth in a girl's ovaries and a boy's testicles. But by stimulating these sex glands to release their sex hormones, they also set off a range of changes very different in boys and girls. The effect of the testosterone released by a boy's testicles and the oestrogen and progesterone released by a girl's ovaries could hardly be more different.

PUBERTY IN GIRLS

Girls may reach puberty at any time between nine and fifteen years old, and sometimes beyond. About eleven seems to be average for North American and European girls. Inside, the ovaries grow to ten times the size they were before and begin to release their sex hormones.

The first visible sign of puberty is often a gentle budding of the breasts and growth of the nipples. In the same year, a girl may notice hair beginning to sprout under her arms and soft down appearing around her genitals. Soon she will begin to grow swiftly and her body subtly changes shape, as hips grow wider and waist slimmer, and breasts round out. But the most significant event is yet to come.

Inside, the development of the sexual organs continues apace as the ovaries and uterus enlarge ready to become reproductive. Then eventually, often around the age of thirteen, a girl experiences her menarche, her first menstrual period (see page 92). To begin with, periods may be erratic, but within a year or so they settle down to a regular 28-day cycle. With the arrival of the regular cycle, she is sexually mature and physically capable of bearing a child.

PUBERTY IN BOYS

In boys, the first obvious signs of puberty appear two or three years later than in girls. Changes may actually start much earlier but they are hard to spot. At around the age of thirteen or fourteen, a boy's testicles will start to grow bigger and his scrotum subtly changes colour and texture. A little later hair

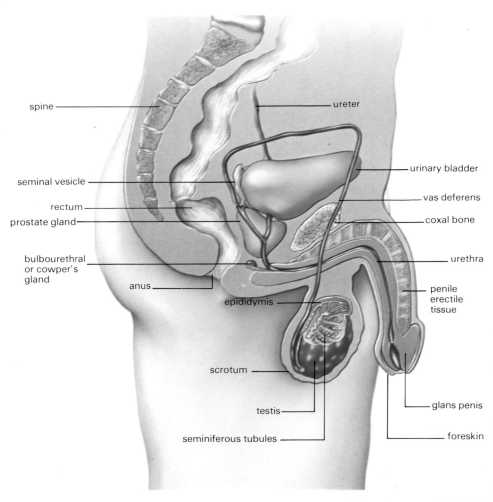

spine

seminal vesicle

rectum

prostate gland

bulbourethral or cowper's gland

anus

epididymis

scrotum

testis

seminiferous tubules

ureter

urinary bladder

vas deferens

coxal bone

urethra

penile erectile tissue

glans penis

foreskin

may start to grow under his arms and around his genitals.

After a year or so, he begins to grow rapidly and may soon overtake a younger girl who may have been taller than him. This growth spurt can be dramatic and

he may grow 10 cm (4 in) in a year or even more.

Soon his penis starts to grow as well. Inside, the sexual organs develop rapidly. The body starts to produce the male sex cells, sperm. Sperm are created by meiosis (see

pages 82–83) in the winding seminiferous tubules in the testicles. The testicles lie outside the rest of the body in the scrotum because sperm production needs a cooler environment than that found inside the body.

Right: In the years immediately after puberty, we become increasingly aware of our sexual identity and relationships with the opposite sex change subtly.

The main elements of the male sexual organs (below left) are: the testicles where sperm is produced in the seminiferous tubules; the vas deferens, the narrow tube that carries sperm; the seminal vesicle and prostate gland which provide a fluid called semen to wash the sperm down the urethra to the penis; and the penis with its erectile tissue. The main elements of the female sexual organs (below) are: the ovaries where eggs are produced; the fallopian tubes that carry the ripened egg to the uterus, where a fertilized egg may grow into an embryo; the narrow cervix leading from the uterus; and the vagina, the muscular tube that accepts the man's penis during sexual intercourse.

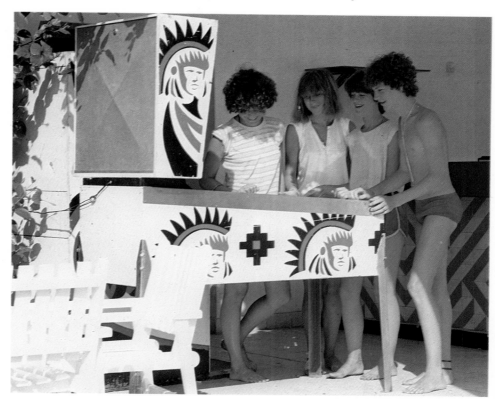

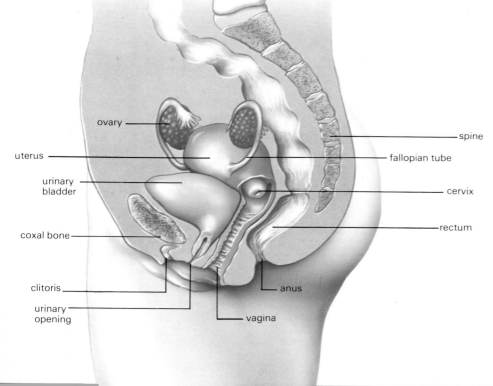

ovary

uterus

urinary bladder

coxal bone

clitoris

urinary opening

vagina

anus

rectum

cervix

fallopian tube

spine

For the first few years of adolescence, a boy's testicles continue to grow and sperm production increases. By the time he is fifteen or so, his body is able to create new sperm at the rate of 200 million a day. Just one of these is enough to fertilize a woman's ova (egg) and create a baby.

Further changes an adolescent male may experience include the appearance of hair on his face and then elsewhere on his body. His voice also deepens and 'breaks' as the larynx grows and doubles the length of the vocal cords. One aspect of adolescence which can be annoying is the increased secretion of oil by the sebaceous glands in the skin. Secretion can be so excessive that pores become clogged and infected, creating spots.

MONTHLY RHYTHMS

From soon after puberty, a woman's body goes through an intricate series of changes every 28 days or so. These changes are usually so regular and predictable that they are called the menstrual cycle, from the Latin word 'mensis' for month.

Menstrual cycles may affect the whole body, but they have one purpose: to prepare an egg for fertilization and the body for pregnancy. Since the egg is only rarely fertilized, each cycle normally ends with the abandoning of the egg and the preparations for pregnancy—ready for a fresh start the next month.

The cycle begins when follicle stimulating hormone (FSH) is released from the front of the pituitary gland.

Unlike male sperm, female sex cells (called oocytes) are ready formed at birth. Each of these cells is held in a little bag or follicle. By the time a girl reaches puberty, there may be half a million follicles still left in the ovaries, but only a few ever become ova (eggs). When FSH reaches the ovaries, it prods perhaps half a dozen of the dormant follicles into action. These follicles spread out around the edge of the ovary and begin to grow. And as

they grow, they begin to secrete the chemical messenger oestrogen.

Travelling through the body in the bloodstream, oestrogen has two important missions. The first is to build up the endometrium (the lining of the uterus) into a rich and cosy bed for a fertilized ovum to settle in. The second is to persuade the pituitary gland to send out another hormone, luteinizing hormone (LH). But levels of oestrogen have to rise considerably before the pituitary will act.

OVULATION AND MENSTRUATION

Meanwhile, in the ovary, one follicle is beginning to assert itself and grow at the expense of the others. When LH finally reaches the ovary, 14 days into the cycle, this follicle is a mature 'Graafian' follicle. The arrival of the LH causes the follicle to burst through the side of the ovary, releasing the ovum (egg). The feathery fingers of the fallopian tube safely grasp the ovum and waft it down the tube towards the uterus. This process is known as ovulation.

The abandoned follicle turns from white to yellow to become a corpus luteum (yellow body). But it goes on sending out oestrogen, and adds a new hormone, progesterone, to its products. This new hormone aids oestrogen in its work building up the endometrium. If the ovum is not fertilized by sperm on its way down the fallopian tube, the corpus luteum finally begins to waste away, after about 22 days of the cycle.

With the disappearance of the corpus luteum, progesterone and

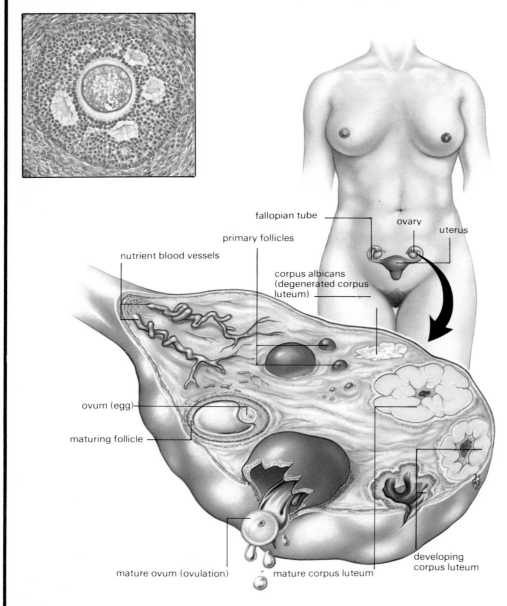

fallopian tube

primary follicles

nutrient blood vessels

corpus albicans (degenerated corpus luteum)

ovary

uterus

ovum (egg)

maturing follicle

mature ovum (ovulation)

mature corpus luteum

developing corpus luteum

Once a month, a new set of follicles begin to develop in the ovaries, stimulated by FSH. They all mature at different rates, and when, two weeks into the cycle, the hormone is produced, only one will be ready (the Graafian follicle) to burst and spill its egg into the waiting fingers of the tubes. The photograph (top left) shows a mature follicle just before ovulation.

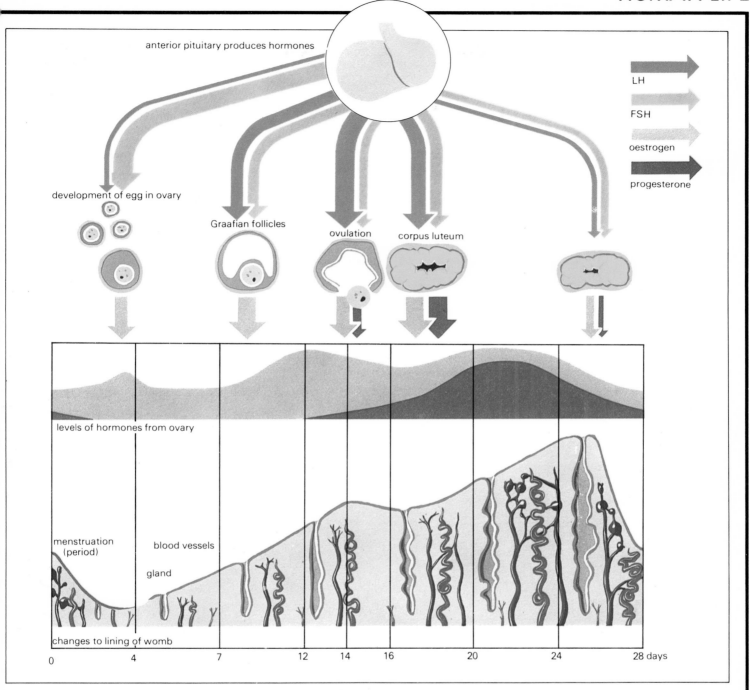

anterior pituitary produces hormones

LH

FSH

oestrogen

progesterone

development of egg in ovary

Graafian follicles

ovulation

corpus luteum

levels of hormones from ovary

menstruation (period)

blood vessels

gland

changes to lining of womb

0   4   7   12   14   16   20   24   28 days

oestrogen levels in the blood begin to drop rapidly. After about 28 days of the cycle, there is too little of these hormones around to keep the endometrium growing. Great chunks of the endometrium begin to break off, releasing blood, fluids, mucus and fragments of uterine lining. This is known as menstruation. The remnants of the endometrium may often flood out through the vagina as menstrual flow. After about five days of menstrual flow, FSH is released

from the pituitary and the cycle starts over again.

If, by any chance, the ovum should be successfully fertilized, the corpus luteum does not waste away. Instead, it grows even bigger and secretes more progesterone and oestrogen. The two hormones help to make the endometrium more and more thick and spongy, ready for the ovum. Soon the fertilized ovum will plant itself in the wall of the uterus. Long after the ovum has settled in and begun to

During the 28 day cycle, there is a regular sequence of interlinked events in the ovaries and uterus, controlled by changing levels of hormones in the blood. The two key hormones are oestrogen and progesterone which control the thickening of the endometrium lining the uterus.

develop, the corpus luteum will go on sending out progesterone to thicken the endometrium and provide plenty of nourishment through pregnancy.

NEW LIFE

For a new human life to be created, the ovum from a woman must be fertilized by a sperm from a man. Only when the 23 chromosomes in each sex cell are united to give the full complement of 46 will a baby begin to develop.

Fertilization can now take place in a test tube. Scientists remove an ovum from the mother's ovaries and unite it with a sperm from the father. Once the egg is fertilized and starts to grow by dividing, it is returned to the mother's womb. This is called 'in vitro' fertilization because it happens in a glass dish—'vitro' is the Latin for glass. But nearly all babies are still conceived 'in vivo' (within the woman's living body) after sexual intercourse, when a man and a woman come together to unite their sex cells.

Sexual intercourse does not always result in conception. The egg can only be fertilized in the 12–24 hours immediately after ovulation, when it is moving slowly down the fallopian tube. So a man's sperm must successfully reach the egg in this short period, roughly half way through the woman's menstrual cycle.

SEXUAL INTERCOURSE

When a man and a woman come together in sexual intercourse, it usually follows a number of physical and social events that improve the chances of a baby being born to loving parents. The culmination of these events is the gentle insertion of the man's penis into the woman's vagina. Back and forth movements of the penis inside

Only a few of the millions of tiny sperms (right) ejaculated from the penis make it all the way to the gigantic ovum (below) and only one may finally penetrate to fertilize the egg (inset).

the vagina produces a series of nervous sensations pleasurable to both man and woman and often leading to a climax of pleasure called an orgasm.

During the man's orgasm, a wave of muscular contractions sweeps 100 million sperms from the testicles to the penis. On their way past the prostate gland and the seminal vesicle, the sperms are joined by a white fluid which helps to carry the sperm onwards. As the

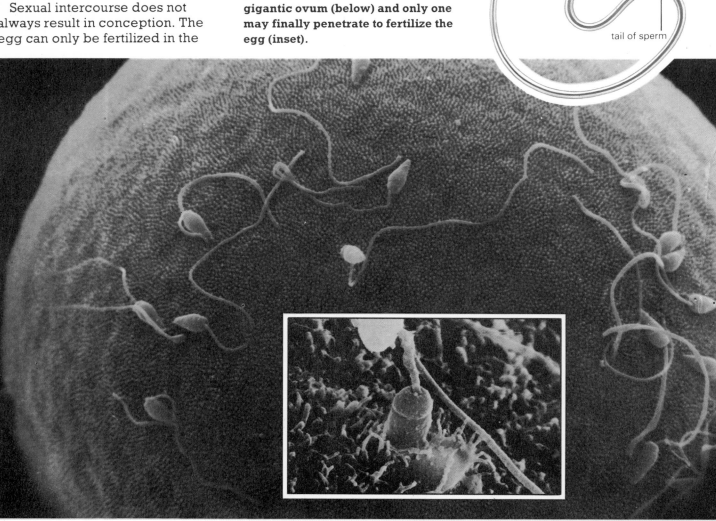

acrosome

head of sperm

mitochondria

midsection of sperm

tail of sperm

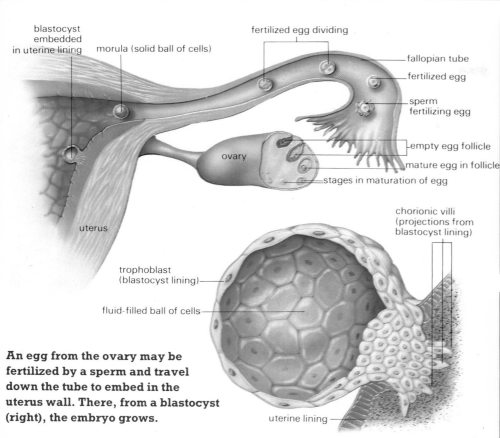

blastocyst embedded in uterine lining

morula (solid ball of cells)

fertilized egg dividing

fallopian tube

fertilized egg

sperm fertilizing egg

empty egg follicle

mature egg in follicle

stages in maturation of egg

ovary

uterus

chorionic villi (projections from blastocyst lining)

trophoblast (blastocyst lining)

fluid-filled ball of cells

uterine lining

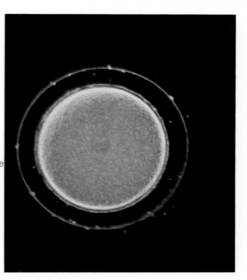

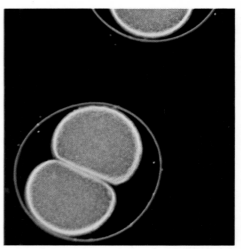

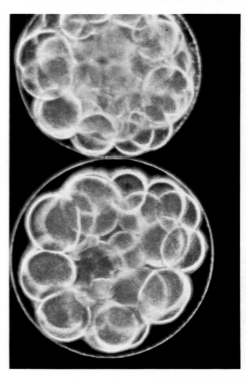

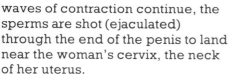

An egg from the ovary may be fertilized by a sperm and travel down the tube to embed in the uterus wall. There, from a blastocyst (right), the embryo grows.

waves of contraction continue, the sperms are shot (ejaculated) through the end of the penis to land near the woman's cervix, the neck of her uterus.

FERTILIZATION

At the cervix, the long and perilous journey of the sperm to meet the ovum really begins. Using its waggling tail to propel it, each of the sperms that have made it as far as the cervix gradually swim up into the uterus. Millions fall by the wayside. The journey across the uterus takes an equally heavy toll. At most, 200,000 reach the far side. When they get there, they must swim up one fallopian tube or the other—but only one contains the ovum. Very few sperm—perhaps between 10,000 and 100,000— choose the right tube, and of these barely 1000 make it to the ovum.

As a sperm approaches the ovum, its head starts to dissolve in chemicals from the ovum. As its protective cap disintegrates, the sperm sends out an enzyme that will

Right: An egg fertilized 'in vitro' grows by cell division before being returned to the mother's womb.

help other sperms penetrate the ovum. It takes enzymes from hundreds of sperms to break down the ovum's protective barrier. Finally just one sperm may succeed in burying its tiny head in the side of the gigantic ovum. As it is engulfed by the ovum, its tail drops off and other sperm are shut out.

Only at this point does the ovum complete the second stage of its meiotic division. The chromosomes of sperm and egg form separate male and female pronuclei. These enlarge and meet in the centre of the egg. The two fuse and they start to divide and grow by mitosis.

In the next 72 hours, the fertilized egg or zygote travels down the fallopian tube into the uterus, growing every hour. As it moves it grows tiny projections that help it burrow into the lining of the uterus as a blastocyst. The uterus then becomes the womb and conception is complete. A new life begins.

PREGNANCY

From the moment of conception until birth some nine months later, the future baby grows steadily in its mother's womb.

When the blastocyst first becomes embedded in the uterus wall, it is a ball of 130 cells or so. Over the next few days, the outer layer becomes distinct from the bud that grows inside near the uterus wall. Soon, tiny fingers on the outer layer (the chorion) begin to burrow their way deep into the wall, preparing the way for the placenta which will both protect and link the embryo to its mother.

Meanwhile, the little bud of cells is beginning to grow away from the chorion on a stalk and separate into two little sacs. One of these buds is the yolk sac; the other is the amniotic sac. The amniotic sac eventually becomes the thin transparent bag, filled with amniotic fluid, that completely envelops the embryo throughout pregnancy.

Four weeks after conception, the embryo is barely bigger than a grain of rice. But it is possible to identify the beginnings of a head and a heart and a tadpole-like tail—there are even bumps that will become arms and legs.

After three months, though, the embryo, now called a foetus, is recognizably human. It already has the main internal organs, dark eye patches and fingers and toes.

At five months, the foetus has grown to almost 25 cm (10 in) long and floats freely in its large capsule of amniotic fluid. Like a warm water bed, the amniotic fluid cushions the foetus from bumps and jolts and protects it from changes in temperature.

After seven months or so, the foetus is small but essentially complete. If for some reason it has to be born at this time, prematurely, it may well survive and grow

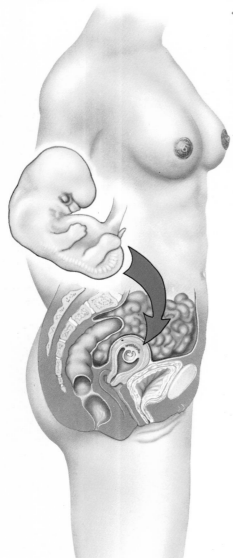

In the safety of the mother's womb, a new human life develops from a few cells to embryo (left) to foetus (above) to baby in nine months, growing larger and more recognizably human.

The foetus is kept warm and safe in its little sac of amniotic fluid (right).

By the time the foetus is ready to be born, it has grown so large that it can barely fit theough the birth canal. Powerful automatic muscle contractions in the uterus help to squeeze the baby out through the cervix, but the baby may still need a helping hand as it appears head first.

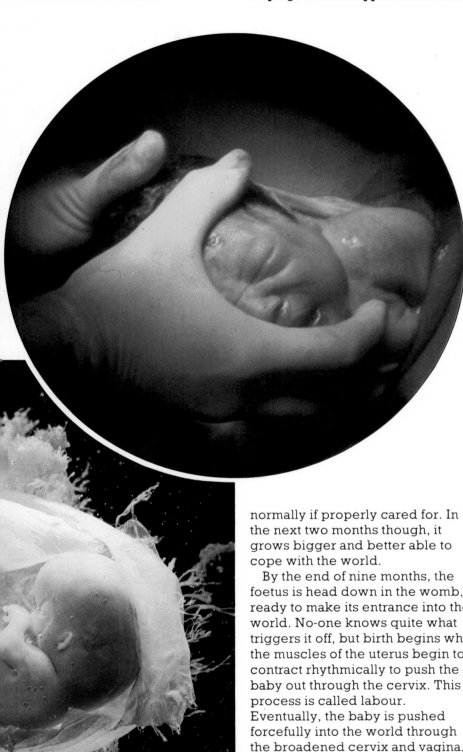

normally if properly cared for. In the next two months though, it grows bigger and better able to cope with the world.

By the end of nine months, the foetus is head down in the womb, ready to make its entrance into the world. No-one knows quite what triggers it off, but birth begins when the muscles of the uterus begin to contract rhythmically to push the baby out through the cervix. This process is called labour. Eventually, the baby is pushed forcefully into the world through the broadened cervix and vagina, together known as the birth canal. When the shock of the new world starts the baby breathing, the umbilical cord linking it with its mother can be cut.

AN INTIMATE RELATIONSHIP

Until the very last weeks of pregnancy, a foetus relies entirely on the blood of the mother for food and oxygen. As the foetus grows, so the mother's body changes to meet its demands. Her blood volume goes up by 30 per cent and so too does her heart rate. Her intake of food begins to increase and she puts on weight rapidly. Surprisingly, even in the later stages of pregnancy, under half this weight is the foetus. The rest of the weight comes from the changes to her body designed to help the foetus and cope with coming motherhood.

Many of these changes are created by the hormones oestrogen and progesterone, so important in conception. Oestrogen, for instance, triggers off enlargement of the breasts and development of the milk glands. Progesterone helps to relax the muscles of the abdomen to allow plenty of room for expansion. At first, the source of the two hormones is the corpus luteum, which is kept going by a special hormone called HCG and another called HCS. HCG and HCS both come from the developing placenta. But once the placenta is fully developed, it starts producing oestrogen and progesterone itself, and the corpus luteum wastes away.

The placenta is a giant-pancake of an organ that develops on the side of the womb and acts as go-between for mother and foetus. The foetus receives its oxygen and food in its mother's blood through its lifeline, the umbilical cord. But every drop of blood the foetus receives from its mother has to pass through the placenta's huge filtration network. This filtration is vital, for the foetus is sensitive to toxins in the blood that the mother can cope with. It is also likely that the placenta protects the foetus from rejection by its mother as foreign tissue.

GROWING OLDER

From the age of 20 on, there is a slow and barely perceptible deterioration of the body machine. The ageing process affects people at different rates, but by the time they are 65 or so, most people are beginning to show all the signs that we associate with old age—grey or white hair, baldness in men, and wrinkled easily bruised skin.

Hair loses its colour because the pigment producing cells stop secreting pigment. Skin becomes wrinkled because the collagen fibres that support the skin begin to stretch. As they stretch they offer less support to the skin and it puckers into wrinkles and folds. Ultraviolet light is believed to accelerate this process. So wrinkles tend to appear first in those parts of the body exposed to the sun—face and hands. A person who spends a great deal of time in strong sunshine may also start to go wrinkly earlier.

There are changes inside the body as well. Some make an older person much less agile and strong. Muscles start to waste and the body becomes generally weaker and bonier. In fact, the number of muscle fibres continually decreases, for as muscle cells die they are not replaced. At the same time, the person may become stiffer in the joints and much more vulnerable to broken bones. This is because as bones age, they lose calcium and become lighter and more brittle. Eventually, an older person may begin to stoop and actually lose a few millimetres in height as the cartilage in between the bones of the back begins to dry out and shrink.

The senses too may begin to dull a little. Eyesight often shows the first signs. Older people may notice spots before their eyes, or that their eyes take longer to adapt to changes in the light than they used to. Eyes tend to become less sharp too, and many older people need glasses.

Then hearing may fade as well, especially at high frequencies—older people are often unable to hear the full range of a good hi-fi system. Men seem to be particularly prone to loss of hearing—perhaps because many have worked in noisier environments all their lives.

Smell and taste may also deteriorate and so can the body's awareness of temperature changes—which is one of the reasons old people are particularly vulnerable to cold.

But most significant of all, perhaps, are changes to the heart and circulation and to the respiratory system. It is the deterioration here that restricts the activity of many people most severely and may contribute to their death.

In old age, blood vessels seem to become particularly prone to atherosclerosis—hardening and narrowing of the arteries by fatty

Over the past century, the age we could expect to live to when we were born has increased dramatically due to advances in treatment and prevention of diseases, sanitation and diet. And as you grow older and survive more and more of the possible dangers, you can expect to live longer and longer.

deposits on the walls. One effect of this is to boost blood pressure. By the time he has reached the age of 70, a man's blood pressure may be 40% higher than it was when he was 25. And because the arteries lose the elasticity which smoothes the flow of blood, there can be wide swings between the diastolic and systolic pressure. All this places a great strain on the heart and makes the person more liable to suffer heart problems.

The narrowing of the arteries can also restrict the flow of blood to the tissues. This can be particularly distressing if it affects the flow of blood to the brain. Restriction of the blood flow may help to make some older people forgetful and easily upset—a condition known as senile dementia.

No-one knows if all these problems are an inevitable part of the ageing process or whether old people just happen to suffer more from them. Indeed, no-one really knows why we grow old at all.

WHY WE GROW OLD

Over the past hundred years, modern medicine, better sanitation and improved diet have helped us to live much longer. In the 19th century, a person could not expect to live much beyond the age of 50. Nowadays, most men expect to live until they are at least 70 and most women until they are at least 76. But we can expect to live longer today, not because the ageing process has been slowed, but because improvements in health help to prevent us dying at an early age. People who remain fit and healthy seem to live no longer—110 years at very most—than they did a hundred years ago.

It seems our lifespan is programmed into us from the moment we are born. Even if we survive accidents and disease, there will inevitably come a time when the body runs out of steam.

Over the past 20 years or so, there has been considerable research to discover just why ageing occurs. Some research suggests that every cell has a built in lifespan programme. Experiments with cells grown in the laboratory showed that cells will only divide 30 to 40 times—only abnormal cancer cells will go on dividing indefinitely. So as more and more of the body cells pass this number of divisions, the body ages because dying cells are no longer replaced.

Another line of research suggests that the genetic coding system of the body is like a record played over and over again. As it is played more and more, it becomes scratched and less reliable.

Evidence gained from children suffering from the rare disease progeria—which makes them look like old people—suggests there might be a chemical pigment called 'lipofuscin' which encourages ageing.

All these ideas are as yet only in the formative stage and it may be we will never discover quite why we grow old.

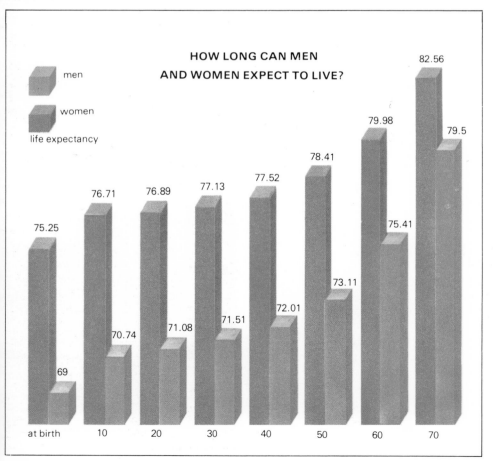

HOW LONG CAN MEN AND WOMEN EXPECT TO LIVE?

men
women
life expectancy

at birth — 75.25, 69
10 — 76.71, 70.74
20 — 76.89, 71.08
30 — 77.13, 71.51
40 — 77.52, 72.01
50 — 78.41, 73.11
60 — 79.98, 75.41
70 — 82.56, 79.5

CHAPTER 7

THE BODY'S DEFENCES

Each human body is just one living organism among countless others in the world. Of these, a whole host are direct rivals to our existence. These infectious microbes are continually trying to invade our bodies, and in order to survive, we need adequate defences against them. The immune system is such a defence system which, with its complexities and unique versatility, is able to defeat most challenges.

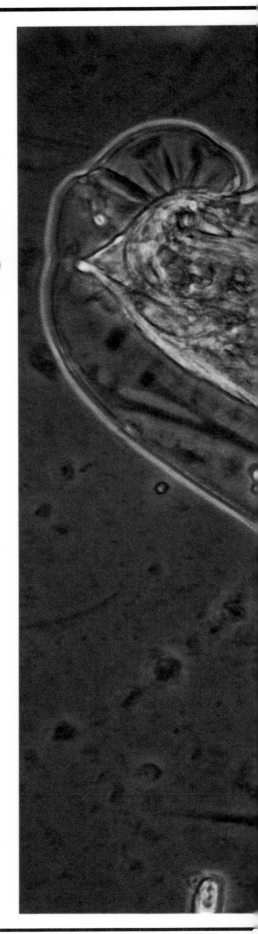

An elaborate system of defences, from an enclosing layer of skin to special antibodies, protect our bodies from minute invaders such as this bacterium.

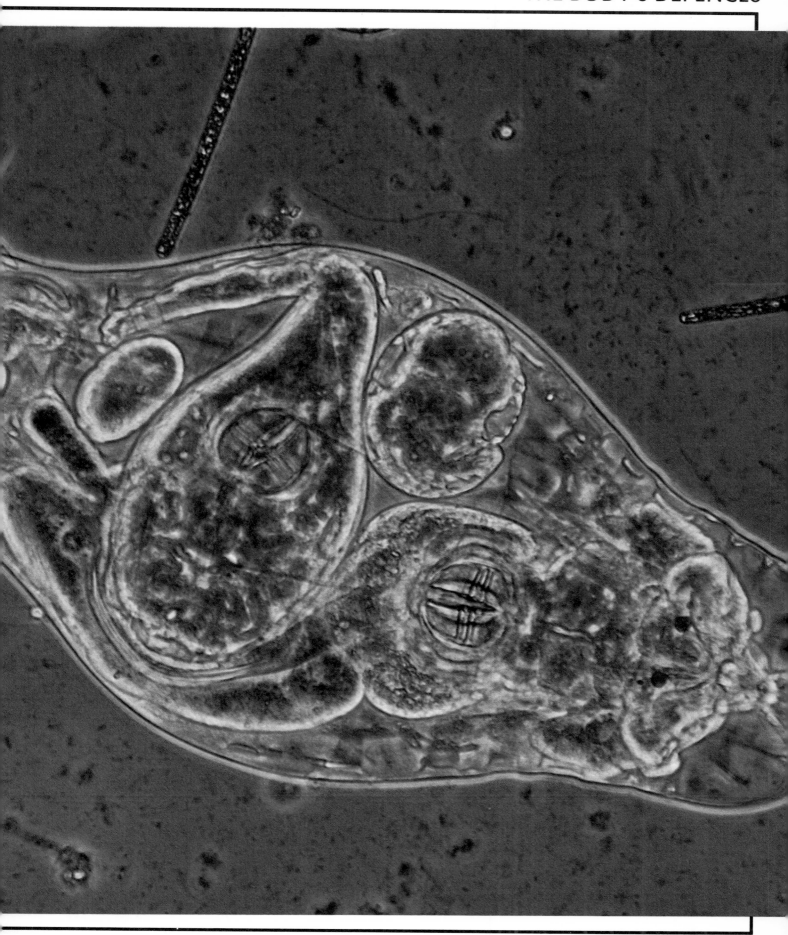

THE SKIN

Skin is the most obvious of all the body's defences. To harm your body physically, something from the outside world has first to get through the protective layer of your skin. Disease microbes, in particular, can do you great damage if they manage to penetrate deep into your body. But in fact countless numbers of bacteria, many kinds of which can cause disease, actually live on your skin without ever getting through it.

SKIN STRUCTURE

Much of this protection is conferred by the outermost layer of the skin, which varies greatly in thickness from under 0.5 mm ($^1/_{50}$ in) on the delicate eyelids, to 6 mm ($^1/_4$ in) or more on the thick soles of the feet. This is called the epidermis, and consists largely of dead, flattened cells that are shed from the body continuously. Flaky dandruff from the skin of the scalp is an obvious example. Only the innermost cells of the epidermis are active and living, and it is they that produce the outer cells, which flatten and die as they near the skin surface.

Just below the epidermis are special cells that produce a pigment called melanin, which protects the body from the harmful effects of ultraviolet rays in sunlight. In absorbing these harmful rays, melanin turns a deeper shade of brown.

Deeper still is the usually thicker skin layer called the dermis. This is also much more varied than the epidermis because it contains many kinds of cells and many-celled structures. Hairs, which (in animal bodies at least) help to protect the body from cold, are rooted in the dermis, although the cells of the hair-pits actually come from the epidermis. Surrounding the hair roots are the sebaceous glands, which make an oily substance that protects skin and hair by keeping them healthily supple. Deeper in the dermis are the sweat glands, which assist in keeping the body cool by evaporation of sweat from its surface. Sweat also has another important protective function—it helps carry away poisonous wastes made inside our bodies. Skin, therefore, is also a major organ of excretion.

The skin is made up of two different layers of tissue: the dermis and epidermis. Both layers contain nerve endings which transmit sensations of pain, pressure, heat and cold. The sweat glands are vital in regulating the body's temperature, while the sebaceous glands lubricate the skin and hair.

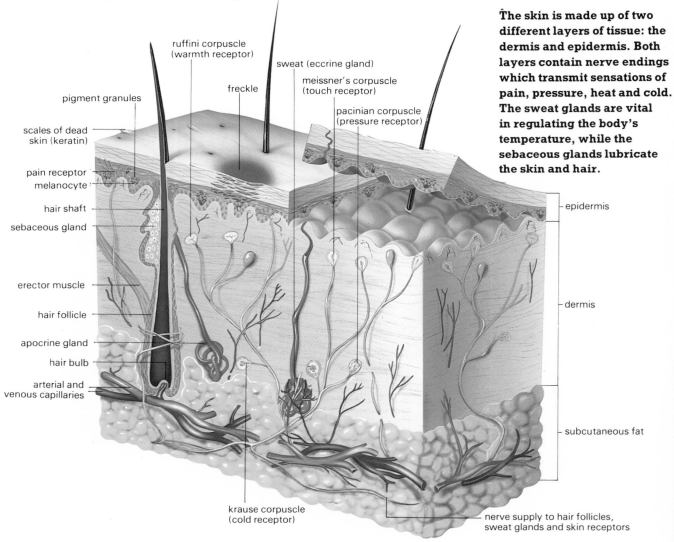

pigment granules

scales of dead skin (keratin)

pain receptor
melanocyte

hair shaft

sebaceous gland

erector muscle

hair follicle

apocrine gland

hair bulb

arterial and venous capillaries

ruffini corpuscle (warmth receptor)

freckle

sweat (eccrine gland)

meissner's corpuscle (touch receptor)

pacinian corpuscle (pressure receptor)

epidermis

dermis

subcutaneous fat

krause corpuscle (cold receptor)

nerve supply to hair follicles, sweat glands and skin receptors

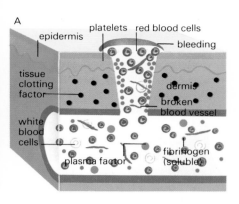

A

epidermis   platelets   red blood cells

bleeding

tissue
clotting
factor

dermis

broken
blood vessel

white
blood
cells

plasma factor

fibrinogen
(soluble)

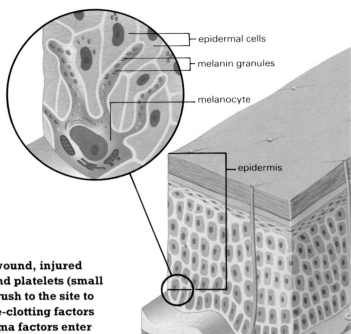

epidermal cells

melanin granules

melanocyte

epidermis

Right: Melanin granules are produced in the epidermis by cells called melanocytes. Exposure to sunlight speeds up the action of the melanocytes which protect the body from harmful light rays.

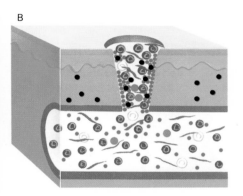

B

Left: In the case of a wound, injured blood vessels bleed and platelets (small sticky cells in blood) rush to the site to help seal it (A). Tissue-clotting factors are released and plasma factors enter the area (B). The reaction of the platelets, both types of factors and other clotting agents convert fibrinogen (a protein) into strands of fibrin. This becomes a jelly-like mesh across the break (C). Platelets and blood cells are trapped in this mesh which now recedes, oozing out serum which helps form a scab (D). This will prevent bacteria entering the body and causing an infection.

already living on the skin, can get through it to set up disease. The way this happens, and the way the body fights it, you can read about on the following pages. Meanwhile, even if no bacteria or other harmful microbes have penetrated the wound, blood is flowing from it and needs to be stopped if the body is not to be weakened. How does the body manage this?

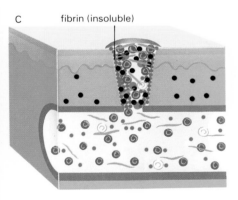

C

fibrin (insoluble)

Part of our body's defence system is the ability to detect heat, cold, pain and touch or pressure. The nerve endings for all these vital sensations are situated in the dermis. So too are many small blood vessels that bring nourishment to all the different kinds of living cells in the skin layers. The deepest or innermost of skin layers is composed mostly of fatty cells. In we non-hairy human beings, it is this layer that is the insulating blanket that most protects our bodies from cold.

The full answer is a very complicated one because many different cells and complex substances in the blood are involved, in a chain reaction that leads eventually to the formation of a protective blood clot. Briefly, the blood oozing from a wound quickly becomes jelly-like because countless numbers of tiny fibres begin to form in it. They tangle up with blood cells and at the same time contract in length to trap the cells tightly. This squeezes out serum, the liquid part of the blood, accounting for the moistness of a newly-formed scab. This scab soon dries up and effectively plugs the wound. Later on, as new skin forms over the wound area, the scab is no longer needed and is dissolved away by further complicated blood substances.

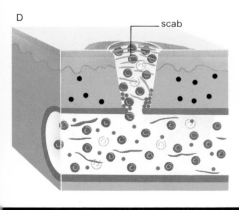

D

scab

SKIN REPAIR

Skin is our vital outermost protection—but what if this protection is breached, say by a weapon or other sharp instrument? Then, harmful bacteria, perhaps

FIGHTING INTRUDERS

On the previous pages we saw how a skin wound heals healthly and normally by formation of a scab. If the wound has become infected by harmful microbes, however, it is a different story. Because of the infection, the skin may not heal so easily. The commonest way in which this can happen is by penetration of the skin through a small wound—say a pin-prick—by bacteria called staphylococci, which live quite harmlessly on the skin surface. When these enter the wound, they quickly multiply in the deeper skin tissues to set up the painful sort of inflammation we call a boil. This swells up and eventually bursts to release a quantity of yellow pus, after which the boil usually goes away, although a 'grumbling' infection can produce a whole crop of boils before it finally dies down.

That it *does* die down, in most cases, shows that the body's defence system has dealt with the infection effectively to produce a cure—to win the battle against the invaders. Like scab-formation in wound healing, this is a very complicated process involving many different kinds of body cells and substances.

As cells around the wound are damaged or killed—either by the wound itself or the bacterial attack—they send out cries for help, releasing special chemicals into the surrounding tissue fluid. The most important of these chemicals is histamine. It is the release of histamine that provokes the inflammation.

Histamine causes inflammation in a number of ways. First of all, it widens the blood vessels around the affected area to boost the blood supply. Secondly, it makes the walls of the blood vessels more permeable so that plasma proteins and white blood cells can stream into the tissue fluid to attack the intruders. The chemicals released by the damaged cells also draw in the body's armoury of defending cells —a process called chemotaxis.

First on the battlefield are usually the white blood cells called neutrophils or polymorphs(see page 21), which roam through the blood

Below: When a splinter introduces bacteria to the skin, white blood cells rush in to the defence.

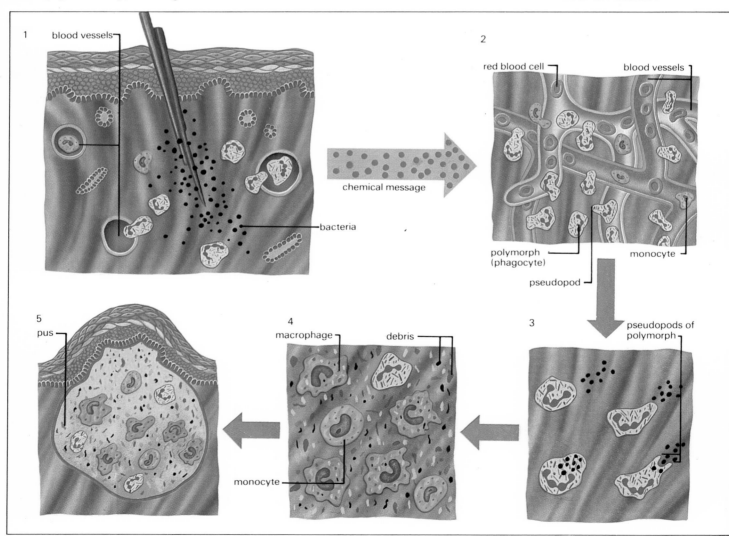

1 blood vessels

chemical message

bacteria

2 red blood cell — blood vessels

polymorph (phagocyte)

monocyte

pseudopod

3 pseudopods of polymorph

4 macrophage — debris

monocyte

5 pus

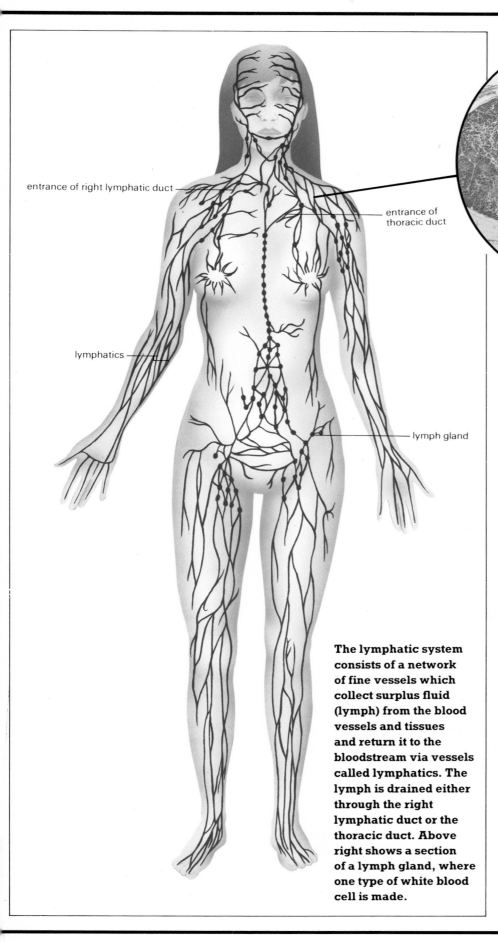

entrance of right lymphatic duct

entrance of thoracic duct

lymphatics

lymph gland

The lymphatic system consists of a network of fine vessels which collect surplus fluid (lymph) from the blood vessels and tissues and return it to the bloodstream via vessels called lymphatics. The lymph is drained either through the right lymphatic duct or the thoracic duct. Above right shows a section of a lymph gland, where one type of white blood cell is made.

in search of debris and intruders. These are phagocytes—cell eaters. When they reach the sight of infection, they engulf any bacteria they encounter. Sometimes the bacteria survive inside the cell; sometimes enzymes in the cell destroy the bacteria—but in killing the bacteria, the cells kill themselves. It is the dead white cells around the infected site that make up much of the pus.

A little while later, a second kind of phagocyte arrives, the giant macrophages (called monocytes when they are in the blood). Like the polymorphs, they are drawn towards the infected area by chemotaxis and, once there, engulf bacteria. A single macrophage can swallow 100 or so bacteria.

THE LYMPHATIC SYSTEM

Should the bacteria overwhelm the defending cells, the body has a second line of defence in the body's lymphatic system. The lymphatic system is a network of fine capillaries that acts as a drainage system for the tissue fluid. The lymph ducts collect the fluid from the spaces between the cells and channel it back into the blood circulation. But before the lymph fluid can travel far, it usually meets a lymph node which contains a concentration of the body's defence cells and effectively filters out microbes that have made it past the first line of defence.

ANTIGENS

Whenever a foreign particle or substance enters or penetrates the body, this is likely to make the body react against the foreigner to save itself from harm. We have already seen how the body's defence system reacts to the invasion of bacteria through a wound in the skin.

There are, of course, other ways in which microbes or foreign substances can enter the body. For example, they can be breathed in with the air we take into our lungs, or eaten or drunk with our meals. And the number of possible foreign invaders is almost without limit. Think of all the different bacteria, viruses and other microbes that surround us in air, water and soil. Then think of the countless other foreign particles we are likely to take into our bodies, in such forms as fumes, dust and pollen grains. It is not so surprising that the body's

immune system should be so very complicated, when it has to deal with all these different invaders.

One of the most remarkable features of the body's defensive system is that it works on two levels against certain types of invader—notably bacteria and viruses. These germs are not only assaulted by the general range of defenders deployed in the way described on the previous page. They are also assaulted by a range of defensive mechanisms that can be targeted on each particular kind of germ. Any germ that provokes this tailor-made assault is called an antigen, and the tailor-made assault is usually referred to as the immune response.

Central to the body's immune response are special blood cells called lymphocytes. There are many different types of lymphocyte, each

with its own particular role to play, but they fall into two main categories: B lymphocytes and T lymphocytes. There are concentrations of these cells in the lymph nodes, which is why the nodes are so important in the body's defence, but they can also move to the site of an infection when the alarm is raised.

It is the B lymphocytes that are responsible, ultimately, for the production of antibodies, one of the key weapons in the fight against invaders. There are millions and millions of groups of slightly different B lymphocytes, each equipped with antibodies designed to fight a specific antigen.

When an antigen comes into contact with a B lymphocyte with matching antibodies, the lymphocyte reacts by dividing in two. One cell becomes a 'memory' cell which circulates in the blood, preparing the body for a

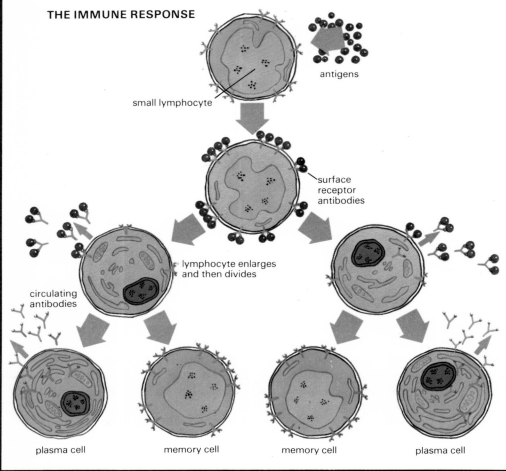

THE IMMUNE RESPONSE

antigens

small lymphocyte

surface receptor antibodies

lymphocyte enlarges and then divides

circulating antibodies

plasma cell

memory cell

memory cell

plasma cell

Right: A pollen grain, greatly enlarged. Pollen can cause an allergic response in people who suffer from hay fever.

Left: When bacteria or other foreign invaders manage to get into our bodies, they cause a defence reaction called the immune response. Cells of the body make chemical antibodies which attack the invaders by binding to the chemical antigens on their surface. Even a few such invaders, with only a small number of antigen molecules, can cause the body to produce a host of antibody molecules, which then defend the body against any further major attack by the particular invader, and in this way prevent disease. This immune response first involves the recognition of the invader antigen by a body cell called a lymphocyte. This then divides and multiplies and passes on its knowledge of the antigen to its daughter cells. Some of these become lymphocytes and plasma cells that produce large amounts of antibody required to fight the invader. Other daughter cells become memory cells which can, if necessary, produce a still further, fast, attacking response to the particular foreign invader of the body.

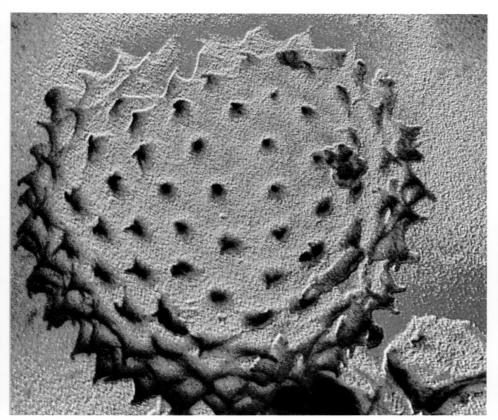

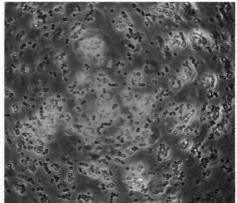

Below: Staphylococcus bacterium inhabits the nasal passages and the skin. It is usually harmless.

Bottom: Sophisticated staining techniques are used to follow antibody/antigen reactions. In the picture on the left human cells infected with Herpes virus are stained yellow in the presence of the Herpes antibody. The same antibody does not have any effect on the colour of non-infected cells (right).

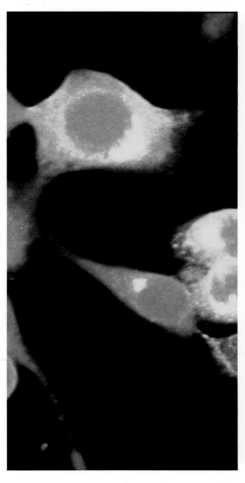

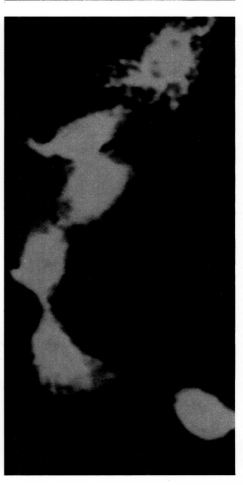

second invasion by the same antigen —which is why we rarely catch the same disease twice. The other cell develops into a special plasma cell, which is a factory for antibody. The new antibodies attack the invaders in a variety of ways— mainly by making them vulnerable to the roaming scavenger cells.

Before antigens match with the B lymphocytes, they must usually be 'presented' by special kinds of T lymphocytes called helper cells— though some B lymphocytes can manage without this personal introduction. But there are other types of T cell that can go directly into action against invaders themselves, without the aid of antibodies. Some of these cells can kill body cells infected by virus—the virus can otherwise multiply safely inside these cells. Others trigger all kinds of defence mechanism into action.

Both antibodies and T cells are aided by an arsenal of special chemicals and cells, and the body can combat an enormous range of infections with its immune system.

TYPES OF IMMUNITY

Immunity means freedom from danger or unpleasantness, and the body's defence system or immune system helps free us from the attack of disease. Like a vastly numerous chemical army, it is on guard at all times against microbes that would otherwise threaten our bodies with dangerous infections.

NATURAL IMMUNITY

We get our first immune protection from our mothers, who give us a stock of protective antibodies. But after a few weeks of life outside the womb, we begin to make our own antibodies. This is the direct result of our being exposed to the outside world that contains so many kinds of microbes. Their different antigens cause our bodies to make antibodies against them, so that we are protected against any further major attacks.

Some types of microbes, however, manage to settle down and live in our bodies. They help defend their new homeland by keeping out less pleasant foreigners. Some of these normal flora, as they are called, even help make vitamins and other substances necessary for our bodies.

So far, so good. Our bodies have developed their defence system, antibodies, normal flora and all, to

Lymphocytes are the body cells most closely concerned with immunity. They are produced by mother cells in such parts of the body as the bone marrow. B lymphocytes are the cells that give rise to a range of antibodies for directly attacking microbes or other invaders of the body. T lymphocytes are cells that attack invaders that have learned to live inside body cells, out of reach of antibodies. By killing such infected body cells, T lymphocytes also get rid of the invading parasites.

Lymphokines are substances made by a range of cells also produced by the bone marrow, which help in this process. Some lymphokines can kill cells infected by viruses, while others help or suppress the action of T lymphocytes, as required.

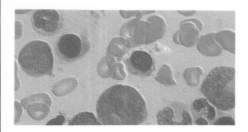

A microscopic view of B lymphocytes in the blood.

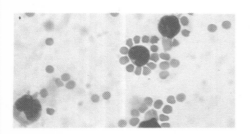

A microscopic view of T lymphocytes.

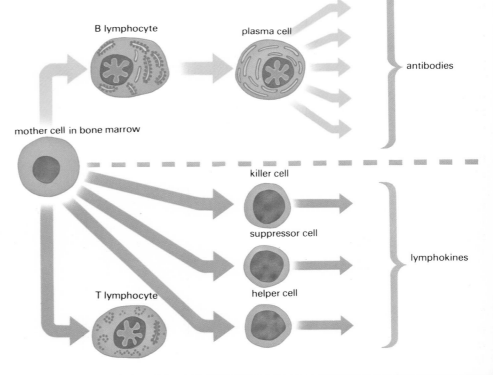

B lymphocyte → plasma cell → } antibodies

mother cell in bone marrow

killer cell →
suppressor cell →
helper cell → } lymphokines

T lymphocyte

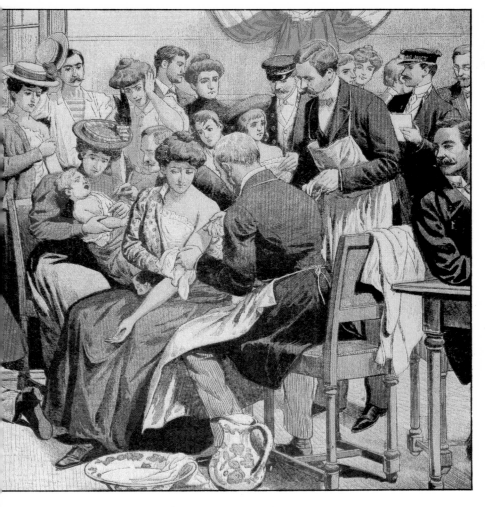

Left: Vaccination against smallpox has been practised since Victorian times. The vaccine consists of harmless cow pox virus, which is very similar to smallpox.

antibodies required, but these have been made, or raised, not in our own bodies but in those of laboratory animals. It protects us usually for a few months only, after which we need another shot of protective antibodies if we are still exposed to the infection.

TROUBLE WITH IMMUNITY

Because the immune system is so very complex it would be all the more surprising if it worked perfectly at all times. One of the chief ways in which it goes wrong is mistaking cells and tissues of our own bodies for strangers or intruders, then proceeding to attack these parts of our bodies, mainly with the aid of T lymphocytes and other killer cells shown in the diagram. In this way the immune system actually makes us ill, by causing autoimmune diseases, such as various severe forms of arthritis in which the killer cells attack the joints of our bodies.

Any hospital patient who has had an organ transplant or a skin graft is a more legitimate target for attack by his own immune system, which cannot know that the new addition is necessary to his well-being, so attacks it like any other stranger.

keep us free from infectious disease. Unfortunately, life is neither so simple nor so perfect. For one thing, most people in the world are not as fit as they might be, because of undernourishment and bad and insanitary housing. This means that they are both exposed to more infection, and also have less resistance to it. Additionally, childhood infections that are common all over the world, such as colds, measles and some kinds of diarrhoea, do little harm in well-off and well-fed countries, while helping to kill hundreds of thousands of children each year in poor and badly-fed countries.

CONFERRED IMMUNITY

The risk of our suffering badly from an infection—including any common childhood one—is made far less if we are given immune protection in the form of a vaccine or an antiserum. A vaccine contains the infectious microbe itself, either killed or much reduced in virulence or dangerousness. It arouses our immune system to make antibodies, so giving us protection for any period from a month or two, to a whole lifetime. An antiserum contains the actual

Fact file . . .

The body's natural defence system includes skin, which is a barrier against invading microbes, and the immune system, which fights any that do get in.

Sometimes we need added protection: vaccines to arouse antibodies, or antisera to provide them.

INDEX